R.GOSCINNY—

Asterix

ADVENTURE GAMES
OPERATION BRITAIN

Illustrated by Uderzo

HODDER AND STOUGHTON
LONDON SYDNEY AUCKLAND

Other exciting titles in the Hodder and Stoughton Adventure Game Books series are:

FAMOUS FIVE ADVENTURE GAMES:

THE WRECKERS' TOWER GAME
THE HAUNTED RAILWAY GAME
THE WHISPERING ISLAND GAME
THE SINISTER LAKE GAME
THE WAILING LIGHTHOUSE GAME
THE SECRET AIRFIELD GAME
THE SHUDDERING MOUNTAIN GAME
THE MISSING SCIENTIST GAME

ASTERIX ADVENTURE GAMES:

ASTERIX TO THE RESCUE
OPERATION BRITAIN

THE PETER PAN ADVENTURE GAME:

PETER'S REVENGE

BIGGLES ADVENTURE GAMES:

THE SECRET NIGHT FLYER GAME
THE HIDDEN BLUEPRINTS GAME

THE FOOTBALL ADVENTURE GAME:

TACTICS!

GHOST ADVENTURE GAMES:

GHOSTLY TOWERS
GHOST TRAIN

WHO-DONE-IT ADVENTURE GAME:

SUSPECTS!

BATTLE QUEST:

CAVES OF FURY
TUNNELS OF FEAR

British Library Cataloguing in Publication Data

Goscinny
    Operation Britain.—(Asterix adventure games/Goscinny).
    1. Adventure games—Juvenile literature
    I. Title   II. Uderzo
    793'.9   GV1203

    ISBN 0-340-41324-7

First published 1987
Eighth impression 1992

Compiled by Anthea Bell and Derek Hockridge

Published by Hodder and Stoughton Children's Books,
a division of Hodder and Stoughton Ltd,
Mill Road, Dunton Green, Sevenoaks, Kent TN13 2YA

Photoset by Rowland Phototypesetting Ltd,
Bury St Edmunds, Suffolk

Printed in Great Britain by BPCC Hazells Ltd
Aylesbury, Bucks, England
Member of BPCC Ltd

It was 50 BC, and Gaul, the country we now know as France, was entirely occupied by the Romans. Well, not entirely . . . one small village of indomitable Gauls, in the province of Armorica, now called Brittany, still held out against the invaders. And life was not easy for the Roman legionaries who garrisoned the fortified camps of Totorum, Aquarium, Laudanum and Compendium . . .

The Gauls who lived in that one little village were brave and tough, fond of food and drink and a bit of fun. And the best fun they could think of was thumping Romans. Roman garrison after Roman garrison came out to the fortified camps, hoping to defeat the villagers – because then, and only then, would Caesar really be conqueror of all Gaul. Roman garrison after Roman garrison had to admit failure and go back to Rome, hoping against hope they could avoid a date with the lions in the Circus Maximus.

The cunning little warrior Asterix, and his great friend Obelix the menhir-delivery man, have already triumphed many times in the Gauls' struggle against the Romans. This time, YOU can help them! Using the cards and equipment provided with this Game Book, you can guide them on their latest adventure, which has been code-named OPERATION BRITAIN. It's up to you whether they succeed or fail.

There's more than one way you can help them to reach the end of the adventure and carry out their mission – and you may not be successful first time. If you aren't, try another route, or select a different item of equipment. And once you *have* succeeded, using your skill at making decisions, and whatever luck comes your way, you can always play the game again and see if you can find another way for the Gauls to win through against the Romans.

HOW TO PLAY

Asterix and Obelix need your help if they are to succeed in their mission, code-named OPERATION BRITAIN.

Start by reading PARAGRAPH ONE, follow the instructions at the end of it, and then go on from paragraph to paragraph as directed. Either you will reach the end of the mission successfully, or you will find that you and the two Gauls (with Obelix's faithful hound Dogmatix) are unable to complete it this time. Then you can go back to the beginning and play the game again.

You will find you are quite often asked to make up your mind between several choices – which is the best road to take, or what is the right password to use? You may be holding an ITEM of equipment which tells you the correct answer – if not, you will have to guess. There are four ITEMS available: a coinbag, a map, a little word-list called a translator, and a password scroll. You can choose just one ITEM to take with you when you begin the game, but you may be told to pick others up later. Keep all the ITEMS you hold in the waist-slit of the OBELIX CARD. Whenever you have consulted an ITEM you are holding, remember to return it to the OBELIX CARD. Then you can tell at a glance which useful ITEMS you have available to help you in the game.

Any ITEMS you do not hold, and which are not in the waist-slit of the OBELIX CARD, **must not be used or consulted** until the game reaches a point where you are told to pick them up.

Asterix has some gourds of magic potion with him, represented by the MAGIC POTION CARDS. Keep them in the waist-slit of the ASTERIX CARD. Whenever he drinks a gourd of potion to help him during the adventure, you must remove a MAGIC POTION CARD from the waist-slit of the ASTERIX CARD. When Asterix has no magic potion left, he will not be able to go on with the adventure, so you will have to start the game again. You could try choosing a different ITEM to start with next time.

OPERATION BRITAIN BEGINS

The Romans knew that the secret of the Gauls' success was the magic potion brewed by Getafix the village druid, which gave them superhuman strength. They had often tried to capture Getafix, hoping to get the secret of the potion out of him, but Asterix and Obelix had rescued him every time.

The origin of this potion was lost in the mists of time . . . it had been handed down from druid to druid by word of mouth. All Getafix could reveal was that there was mistletoe and lobster in it . . . the lobster was optional, but it improved the flavour.

The mistletoe, however, was not optional! It was a vital ingredient. And now it looked as if Nature had come to the aid of the Romans. Disaster had struck – the mistletoe crop had failed all over Gaul!

Chief Vitalstatistix was at his wits' end. Even Getafix had no answer to the problem – stocks of potion were running low, and without mistletoe he couldn't make a fresh supply. There was just one hope: a message had come from Asterix's British cousin Anticlimax, to say that there was a good mistletoe crop in Britain. Mistletoe for the potion should really be cut by a druid using a golden sickle . . . but as Chief Vitalstatistix couldn't spare Getafix himself, Asterix, Obelix and Dogmatix volunteered to go to Britain and bring back a sackful. And Getafix sent messages by pigeon post to his druid friends in Britain, asking them to cut the mistletoe for the Gauls when they came. For special, magic mistletoe, the kind he needed, grew in only three British oak-woods: one near Londinium, one west of the Caledonian border (Caledonia was the country we now call Scotland), and a third on the island of Mona, now Anglesey.

But Operation Britain would be dangerous. Britain too was under Roman rule, except for the village where Cousin Anticlimax lived. The Gauls had been there before, and if they were recognised while in Britain, the Romans would be keen to capture them. And little did they know that news of their mission had already leaked out . . . for a Roman spy, snooping round the village fence, had overheard their plans.

Luckily there was enough magic potion left for Getafix to give

Asterix some for the journey. Obelix didn't need any; he had fallen into the cauldron of potion when he was a baby, and it had a permanent effect on him. Getafix also offered the two heroes a map of Britain, showing a number of British towns and other landmarks, and a small marble tablet with a list of foreign words on it, called a translator, to help them understand people who spoke foreign languages. Vitalstatistix offered them a bag of coins, which he felt sure would be useful, and a scroll he had picked up during a raid on the camp of Aquarium, giving all the passwords in use in the Roman Empire.

But Asterix and Obelix wanted to travel light. They said they would take only one item with them, and hope to get hold of the others as and when they needed them.

Which ITEM do you think they ought to choose – the coinbag, the password scroll, the map of Britain, or the translator? Put whichever of these four ITEMS you have picked into the waist-slit of the OBELIX card. Keep the other three items out of play until you are told to use them.

ASTERIX also has either one, two or three gourds of MAGIC POTION with him. It is up to you to choose how many. The more gourds he has, the easier you will find it to help him complete his mission successfully. If he has all three MAGIC POTION CARDS, you have more chances, and the game will be easier. If you would like to make the game harder, give him only two cards, or for a really difficult mission, only one. Whenever Asterix drinks one of his MAGIC POTIONS, you will be told to remove a card from his waist-slit, and when he has none left, the adventure is over, and you will have to start again from the beginning.

You can make the game depend on your own decision-making **skill** instead of **chance** if, instead of using the special DICE when you are told to throw it, you make up your own mind which of the three possible ways it might fall would be best for the success of OPERATION BRITAIN.

'Now, have you got everything?' asked Getafix. 'Magic potion for Asterix – fresh supplies of tea for our British friends? Goodbye, and bring back all the magic mistletoe you can.' Everyone wanted to wish Asterix, Obelix and Dogmatix luck, and the village street was crowded – until Cacofonix the bard cleared his throat and struck his lyre. 'Here, what's this?' asked Fulliautomatix the village blacksmith. 'A tune, of course,' said the bard. 'You could have fooled me,' muttered Fulliautomatix, taking a good grip on his hammer. 'I will now,' said Cacofonix, ignoring him, 'give you a farewell ode in twenty verses entitled *See The Conquering Heroes Go.*' But by the end of the first verse Asterix and Obelix were haring down the road, the other villagers had run for cover, and Fulliautomatix made sure the first verse was also the last. 'Phew!' said Asterix, once out of earshot. 'Britain will hold no terrors for us after that! We're on the road for Portus Itius, to cross the Mare Britannicum . . . the only question is, how? I suggest we hire a little jolly-boat. We want to be inconspicuous.' 'Do we?' said Obelix. 'I'd like to go in a Roman galley – we could borrow one at Portus Itius,' he added. 'I don't know about that,' said Asterix, doubtfully. 'A merchant vessel might be a better bet.' Dogmatix barked, as if to say he'd like that. 'Though I'd still prefer the jolly-boat,' said Asterix. 'And here's Portus Itius, so we'd better make up our minds.'

Throw the special DICE to decide who chooses the way to cross the Mare Britannicum.

If you throw ASTERIX   go to 262
If you throw OBELIX   go to 129
If you throw DOGMATIX   go to 182

'Nice little place Encyclopaedicus Britannicus has here!' said Obelix. Of course there were sentries on guard outside the Governor's palace. 'We've got no time to lose,' Asterix decided. 'We know for sure that news of Operation Britain has leaked out, so the Romans will be looking out for us. I suggest we bluff our way into the palace, and fast!' He went up to the guards at the gates, and tried an excuse which had worked there once before. 'We're plumbers. Encyclopaedicus Britannicus has got a burst pipe, and we're here to mend it,' he said, and they walked in. *Go to 173.*

The two Gauls sat down in the wood to rest, while Dogmatix sniffed hopefully about for rabbits to chase. 'We might as well go a little farther on into the Cantium countryside,' said Asterix. 'And we could look for things to eat that we could take back – stocks of food are running low in the village.' 'Things to eat! Good idea!' said Obelix, brightening. 'That we could take back, I said!' Asterix reminded him, but just then they spotted a patch of mushrooms growing in the wood.

Throw the special DICE to decide who reaches and picks the mushrooms first.

If you throw ASTERIX	go to 158
If you throw OBELIX	go to 191
If you throw DOGMATIX	go to 34

'It's no use,' sighed Asterix. 'We can't make out what the Thracians are saying – well, that's too bad. But don't you think there were rather a lot of Roman soldiers about the town? It looks to me as if they're expecting some sort of military action – very likely against our friends' village! I think that as the Arch-Druid has told us how to get there, we'd better not waste any more time about it. Come on!' *Go to 209.*

Asterix could not give the password – 'But I'm Asterix, from Gaul,' he said, 'and this is my friend Obelix, and his faithful hound Dogmatix. Maybe you've heard of us?' At this, a smile of recognition spread over the fishmonger's face. 'Why, of course!' he said. 'You did wonders for Mykingdomforanos and his men before – and what's your business in Britain this time?' So Asterix told him, adding that they were after information which might help the rebel British village, since Chief Mykingdomforanos feared a Roman attack. 'Very likely,' said Fishcax. 'There's certainly something fishy going on. A lot of Roman troops have passed this way, going to the fortified camp of Chrysanthemum. You could try seeing what you can find out there – but do go carefully! And take this fish with you!' *Go to 171.*

'How frustrating to be held up by a language problem just when we hoped we were at our journey's end!' said Asterix. There was no way they could find out what the Welsh druids were trying to tell them. 'Or not unless there's an interpreter in Deva!' said Asterix suddenly.

By now, several of the people of Deva had come up. 'There *is* an interpreter in town, but he's very ill,' one of them told the Gauls. 'Take him this – it will cure him in no time!' said Asterix, producing a gourd of magic potion and, sure enough, a very healthy-looking interpreter soon turned up. However, his news wasn't nearly so healthy. 'The druids are telling you that, somehow or other, the Governor of Britain learned of your mission,' he said. 'I feared so – I'm sure there was an information leak even before we left Gaul,' said Asterix. 'But what exactly has happened?' 'The druids were forced to harvest their mistletoe by Roman soldiers, who took it to Londinium – and the same thing happened to the mistletoe from the Caledonian oak-wood!' said the interpreter. 'Oh dear!' said Asterix. 'Well, Obelix – no good crying over cut mistletoe! It's back to Londinium for us.'

Remove a MAGIC POTION CARD from ASTERIX'S WAIST-SLIT. Now go to 115. (Remember: when there are no magic potion cards left in Asterix's waist-slit Operation Britain cannot go on, and you must start the game again.)

7

Obelix got his way, and took the oars while Asterix steered. With his great strength, he rowed the other two across the Mare Britannicum in no time. But just as they were approaching the British coast, they saw a vast Roman galley bearing down on them. 'Ahoy there!' shouted Asterix, afraid the galley hadn't seen them and would capsize their boat. Next moment a suspicious-looking Roman centurion was peering over the rail. The ship was taking a company of legionaries back to Gaul after a tour of duty in Britain. 'Just what are a couple of Gauls doing this side of the Mare Britannicum, may I ask?' inquired the centurion. 'Oh, we're only simple Gaulish fishermen – we got carried away by the current,' explained Asterix hastily, 'and now we're looking for the best place to land. Can you tell us where that is?' 'No idea,' said the centurion. 'You'll have to ask Captain Poisonus Oystus here. The only trouble is, Oystus is a native – a native of some Jupiter-forsaken spot where they don't speak Latin *or* Gaulish. You need a translator to make out what he says.'

Is OBELIX carrying a TRANSLATOR? If so, use it to find out what the captain is saying, and follow the instruction in his speech bubble. If not, go to 133 instead.

8

'It's a pity we couldn't understand that man . . . I'm afraid we're going the wrong way,' said Asterix, as they walked on through the crowd. Suddenly there was a shout of recognition. 'My old friends Asterix and Obelix!' It was Ekonomikrisis the Phoenician merchant. 'Ssh!' said Asterix. 'Keep your voice down! Ekonomikrisis, you're the very man we want! Can you give us a lift to Britain? Take us on board, and we'll tell you all about it.' *Go to 206.*

They couldn't pay for the mushrooms – 'And we wouldn't even if we *did* have the money!' said Obelix angrily. 'Mushrooms are free for anybody who likes to pick, and don't you forget it!' He advanced threateningly on the Roman official, who looked terrified. 'No! Don't!' he squeaked. Asterix felt quite sorry for him. 'Stop it, Obelix!' he said. 'This isn't like fighting soldiers, you know!' But Obelix took no notice, even though Dogmatix too was barking away at his heels, as if to say it wouldn't be a fair fight. 'Oh, bother!' said Asterix crossly. 'I'll have to drink some magic potion if I'm to stop him.' Once he *had* taken a dose of potion, he was able to haul Obelix off the frightened Roman, who ran for his life. 'Come on, Obelix,' said Asterix. 'Let's not waste any more time – we're searching for information, remember?'

Remove a *MAGIC POTION CARD* from *ASTERIX'S WAIST-SLIT*. Now go to 255.

'It looks as if we'd better head for Durovernum,' said Asterix, and they started off that way. They had not gone far when they heard someone hailing them. At first they looked round in alarm, fearing they had been recognised by Romans – but next moment they saw an old friend coming down the road towards them. 'By Toutatis, it's Dipsomaniax from the Jug and Amphora pub in Londinium!' cried Asterix. 'Asterix! Obelix! It's good to see you!' said Dipsomaniax warmly. 'But what are you doing in Britain?' The Gauls explained about the failure of the Gaulish mistletoe crop, and Operation Britain. 'I hope we're going the right way for Anticlimax's village; are we?' said Asterix. 'Yes, just carry straight on, and you'll come to the village before this road reaches Durovernum,' said Dipsomaniax. 'In fact, I've just been taking Mykingdomforanos messages from Londinium. You'll have to be careful as you approach the village, though – the Romans have built three fortified camps around it. They're having a big drive to break the villagers' stubborn resistance!' And he told them a path which would get them into the village, avoiding all the Roman camps. 'Here – take this!' added Dipsomaniax, handing them a bag of coins. 'It's from British resistance funds – it may help you on your mistletoe mission, and it's the least we can do after all you did for *us*, when you came here before and taught us how to make tea!'

If OBELIX is not already carrying it, put the COINBAG into his WAIST-SLIT. Now go to 209.

11

The fence around Durobrivae barracks was tall and solid. But all of a sudden, as they walked round it, Dogmatix began barking excitedly and dashed ahead of the others. When Asterix and Obelix reached him, he proudly showed them what he had discovered – a gap in the fence! They could easily slip through – it was big enough even for Obelix. 'And look!' whispered Asterix. 'There's the commanding officer's tent. Let's creep up and see if we can hear anything.' Sure enough, there were voices talking inside the tent. 'Well, Vacuous, my faithful second-in-command?' said one of them. 'Everything ready for the big attack?' 'As ready as it can be, Centurion Outrageous, sir,' said the other. 'Our orders are to crush that little village here in Cantium before the revolting Britons in it can join up with the equally revolting Queen Boadicea,' said Outrageous. 'Then what are we waiting for, sir?' asked Vacuous. 'We're waiting for reinforcements from the nearest big garrison to Londinium,' said Outrageous. 'Those troops are due to arrive from . . .' But all the Gauls could catch after that was the names of three towns – Verulamium, Eboracum and Aquae Sulis. Then trumpets blew, and they thought they had better withdraw. 'If we knew which of those towns is closest to Londinium, we could make a good guess at the length of time it will be before the troops arrive,' said Asterix. 'Have you got a map, Obelix?'

Is OBELIX carrying a MAP? If so, consult it to see which of the towns is closest to Londinium, and follow the appropriate instruction. If not, you must guess which instruction to follow.

If you think it's AQUAE SULIS	go to 64
If you think it's EBORACUM	go to 25
If you think it's VERULAMIUM	go to 202

12

'*WINE* is the password!' said Asterix confidently, to the astonishment of the sentries. 'Well, you've got to let me past now!' he added, as they still hesitated. 'But – but it's against all the rules to let civilians into the Tower! I mean, if we did that they'd be queuing up every day of the week to come and look at the dungeons and the Imperial jewels!' said one of the sentries. 'We won't be long!' Asterix promised. 'Come along, Obelix – what are you waiting for?' 'Just admiring the lovely helmets these two sentries are wearing,' said Obelix. 'Obelix,' said his friend, 'this isn't another helmet-collecting expedition! Help me search the Tower!' But their search was in vain. 'The Imperial jewels are all very well in their way, but doesn't the Governor keep a whole lot of precious mistletoe somewhere?' Asterix asked the sentries when he came out. 'Yes, but not here – it's safe in his palace, so just too bad if you wanted to pinch a sprig or so for your Solstice decorations!' said the sentries, laughing. 'In the Governor's palace, is it?' said Asterix. 'Thanks for telling us!' *Go to 2.*

13

A very showy restaurant caught Obelix's eye. 'That looks good!' he said. To his disappointment, however, when their meal came, it was the same boring old boar as usual in Britain, boiled and served with mint sauce. 'Appearances aren't everything,' said Asterix. 'Never mind, we're not only here for the boar, you know.' When they had finished dinner, they asked the head waiter the way to Caledonia. Unfortunately, though he answered at length, they couldn't understand what he was saying. 'He's from Hispania, I think,' said Asterix. 'Have we got a translator tablet with us, Obelix, to find out what he's saying?'

Is OBELIX carrying a TRANSLATOR? If so, use it to find out what the waiter is saying in the picture below, and follow the direction given in his speech bubble. If not, go to 127.

'Oh, all right, you *do* seem to know the password,' said the large man, grudgingly. 'Yes, it's *CAESAR* in honour of our glorious conqueror!' 'We could tell him a thing or two about his glorious conqueror!' Asterix whispered to his friend, digging him in the ribs, or where he judged the ribs ought to be under all Obelix's padding. 'What was that?' asked the man. 'Oh, nothing – just wondering if any of the glorious conquering troops had been past here recently,' said Asterix. 'Yes, as a matter of fact, they have,' said the man. He was thawing out a bit now. 'Like to see them, would you? Try going up the road to the fortified camp of Delphinium – you ought to catch them there. Here's a map to show you the way.'

If OBELIX is not already carrying the MAP, put it in his WAIST-SLIT. Now go to 160.

Without a coinbag, the Gauls couldn't possibly pay what the Briton was asking – 'And for a meal of boiled boar, at that!' said Obelix. 'Well, could you let us have a boar on credit, and we'll pay you later?' asked Asterix. 'I'm sure my cousin Anticlimax will lend me the money when we meet him.' 'Oho!' said the surly Briton, with a gleam coming into his eye. 'Anticlimax? Isn't he one of those rebels still holding out against the Romans? Come in, come in!' he said, suddenly sounding quite genial. The Gauls came in – and he bolted the front door behind them. 'I know my lodgers would like to meet you – here!' he shouted. 'Some suspicious-looking Gauls for you!' And his lodgers, who had been eating their supper in a back room, appeared – two hefty Roman soldiers. 'Quick!' shouted Asterix. Taking a hasty gulp of magic potion, he overpowered one legionary, while Obelix dealt with the other, and then they both rushed out of the back door with Dogmatix after them. Obelix snatched a leg of boiled boar off one of the lodgers' plates in passing. 'Come on,' gasped Asterix. 'Let's get away from here, fast! This is the road that should take us to Durovernum, and that's the way we want to go.'

Remove a MAGIC POTION CARD from ASTERIX'S WAIST-SLIT. Now go to 72.

'It's no use,' said Obelix. 'We haven't got a translator. This merchant seems friendly, but what he's saying is *still* Greek to me.' 'Or maybe Akkadian,' said Asterix, 'or Phoenician, or Sumerian, or Hittite, or Assyrian, or . . .' 'Well, we can't understand him, anyway, so we'll just have to go on until we meet someone else,' said Obelix. However, before they met anyone else they found out why the foreign merchant had been gesturing in such an excitable way. There was a river in full spate, flooding the road ahead of of them. Obviously the merchant had thought no one could possibly get across. Little did he know what amazing strength the Gauls drew from their magic potion – Asterix drank a dose of it, and as Obelix was permanently under its influence, they had no difficulty in swimming over the turbulent river, with Dogmatix perched on Obelix's helmet. They went on with their journey until they came to a crossroads.

Remove a MAGIC POTION CARD from ASTERIX'S WAIST-SLIT. Now go to 107.

17

Obelix went up to the fishmonger's shop, licking his lips at the sight of the delicious display. 'We'll have the lot!' he said. 'I *beg* your pardon?' said Fishcax. 'I suppose you can pay, can you? If you want the lot, it will cost you seventeen coins!'

Is OBELIX carrying a COINBAG? If so, count out the seventeen coins by rotating the disc, and go to the number given on the other side. If not, go to 151.

They walked on, and after a while they came to a village with a fishmonger's shop in it. 'That reminds me of home!' said Obelix. 'Dear old Unhygienix! I'm so peckish, I could even eat one of the fish *he* sells!' 'Look at the shop sign!' exclaimed Asterix, all of a sudden. 'It says FISHCAX! I've heard of Fishcax – Anticlimax told me to look out for him if we passed his shop. He's not only a fishmonger, he's an undercover agent in the British resistance!' 'So long as he's a fishmonger, that's all I care about,' said Obelix. 'His wares look a little bit fresher than the antiques Unhygienix stocks, too. Let's stop and buy some. We could make a camp-fire in the woods and cook the fish over it.'

Throw the special DICE to decide who is to buy the fish.

If you throw ASTERIX   go to 284
If you throw OBELIX   go to 17
If you throw DOGMATIX   go to 232

19

'No, it's not *MEAD*,' said the Iceni, looking very grim. And out of the fort behind them came something looking even grimmer: a chariot with knives on its wheels. 'You deal with these Britons, Obelix, and I'll see to the chariot!' said Asterix, drinking some magic potion. Obelix was happy to oblige, although he would rather have been thumping Romans. Meanwhile Asterix picked the chariot up, to the astonishment of its driver, so that the knives could do no harm. 'Listen – we really *are* friendly!' he shouted. 'All right!' gasped the leader of the Iceni. 'We believe you – at least, we would if

that big fat man would stop hitting us quite so hard!' 'Fat?' said
Obelix, menacingly, looking far from friendly. 'I didn't mean fat,'
said the Briton hastily. 'He meant well-covered,' said Asterix.
'Well-covered,' agreed the Briton. 'Come into the fort, both of you,
have some mead even though it wasn't the password, and tell
Boadicea your story.'

***Remove a MAGIC POTION CARD from ASTERIX'S
WAIST-SLIT. Now go to 200.***

'I wonder what exactly made Dogmatix so keen on going this way?'
Asterix wondered aloud, as they set off in an easterly direction. He
was soon to find out. Dogmatix had picked up the scent of a
Norman longship cruising along the Mare Britannicum. As the
Normans were very fond of their food, there were all sorts of
delicious meaty left-overs on board the great warship, and that was
what got Dogmatix so excited. But Asterix and Obelix were far from
pleased when the Norman chief, Olaf Timandahaf, turned his ship
to block their way and demanded money to let them pass. 'Let's
fight them!' said Obelix, hopefully, but Asterix thought not. 'It will
be quicker to pay up and get to Britain without delay,' he said. 'Have
you got any money on you, Obelix?' 'We want twenty coins, and
hurry up about it!' ordered the Norman.

***Is OBELIX carrying a COINBAG? If he is, count out twenty
coins by rotating the disc and go to the number shown on the
other side. If not, go to 139.***

The British villager seemed friendly enough when Asterix struck up a conversation with him. 'We're Gaulish tourists,' he said, 'come to see the sights of Britain. I wonder, can you tell us where we'd go to see Roman troops disembarking as they come into the country? That must be a really fine sight!' The villager thought about it. 'I *have* heard of troops landing recently,' he said, 'but I can't quite remember where. Was it Anderida? Or maybe Portus Adurni? Or Dubris? No, it's slipped my mind – though I do recollect a soldier passing through this village telling me it was near the island of Vectis.' 'Hm . . . that's interesting!' said Asterix, thoughtfully. 'Obelix, do you have a map, so that we can find out which seaport is near the island of Vectis?'

Is OBELIX carrying a MAP? If so, use it to find out which seaport is near the island of Vectis, and then follow the appropriate instruction. If not, you must guess which instruction to follow.

If you think it's ANDERIDA	go to 131
If you think it's DUBRIS	go to 27
If you think it's PORTUS ADURNI	go to 253

If anything, the sentry was more baffled than before. He called to a passing officer. 'Centurion Outrageous, sir! Here's this Gaul asking for military information – *and* he's got the correct password, *STAG!* What am I to do, sir?' The centurion looked suspiciously at Obelix. 'You may have the password, but that doesn't give you any right to come inside Roman military installations. Still, I suppose I don't mind if you walk round the outside of the barracks, just to admire the might of Rome from a distance,' he said graciously. *Go to 11.*

23

'We must make for Venta Belgarum,' said Obelix, showing Asterix the map. 'It's still a very long way from the village,' said Asterix. But they were in luck! A smartly-dressed young man in a fast chariot drew up beside them. 'Aren't you Asterix and Obelix, from Armorica?' he asked. 'Surely you remember me – I'm Vitalstatistix's nephew Justforkix!' 'By Toutatis, so you are!' said Asterix, delighted to meet an old friend, and thinking that Justforkix had grown up a lot since his father sent him to Armorica for the Gauls to make a man of him! Obviously, it had worked. . . 'I'm in Britain on business – I went into my father Doublehelix's firm in Lutetia, you know,' said Justforkix. 'Can I give you a lift?' 'Yes, please!' said Asterix, explaining their mission. 'I'll take you straight to the village – nothing easier!' said Justforkix, and off they drove. ***Go to 209.***

Asterix chose a restaurant which was not particularly showy outside, but the food was excellent. There was even roast boar, cooked just as Obelix liked it. 'Less of a bore than most British boar,' he said. 'It's as big a boar as I could get!' said the restaurant proprietor, slightly offended, but Asterix soothed his feelings by explaining what Obelix meant, and he gave Dogmatix a roast wild boarlet all to himself. After their meal, the Gauls wondered where to go next. A signpost pointed to Lindum, Deva and Glevum. 'We want to go north from Ratae, for Caledonia. I wonder which of those towns we should make for? Have you got a map so I can find out?' said Asterix.

Is OBELIX carrying a MAP? If so, use it to find out which of the three towns is north of Ratae, and follow the appropriate instruction. If not, you must guess which instruction to follow.

If you think it's DEVA	go to 155
If you think it's GLEVUM	go to 144
If you think it's LINDUM	go to 86

As the Gauls had no map, they had to guess which of the towns they had heard Outrageous and Vacuous mention was nearest Londinium. 'My guess is Eboracum!' said Obelix. 'I'll just go and find out, shall I?' And before Asterix could stop him, he had gone back round the perimeter fence and was striding into the barracks. 'Hey, you!' he said to the first surprised bunch of Roman soldiers he met inside. 'Where's Eboracum?' 'Eboracum? Oh, miles and miles away, up north!' said one of the legionaries. 'Right,' said Obelix, 'so which is closest, Verulamium or Aquae Sulis?' 'Verulamium, of course,' said the legionary. 'Wait a minute – aren't you one of those Gauls that was hanging around a little while ago? I think you'd better have a word with the centurion!' Hearing the sound of battle inside the barracks, Asterix sighed. 'Oh dear – I suppose I'd better go to Obelix's aid, if we're to get back to Mykingdomforanos in time to help him fight the Romans!' he said, drinking a magic potion.

Remove a MAGIC POTION CARD from ASTERIX'S WAIST-SLIT. Now go to 211.

26

The Gauls sat down to enjoy a really good meal. Even the beer was chilled! 'I could see you were Gauls the moment you came in,' Beeswax the landlord told them, 'and I know Gauls like their beer cold. Just arrived in Britain, have you? Well, you want to be careful if you're on a sightseeing trip – there are Roman patrols everywhere! The Romans are still trying to conquer a little village in Cantium where Chief Mykingdomforanos and his right-hand man Anti-climax are holding out against them. And we in the British resistance movement,' he added, lowering his voice, 'are hoping Queen Boadicea and Mykingdomforanos can join forces! The Romans would do anything to prevent that. Boadicea would be almost as good an ally as the Gaulish heroes Asterix and Obelix who once visited Britain.' Then Beeswax suddenly recognised his guests. 'By Toutatis, I do believe you *are* Asterix and Obelix!' he exclaimed! 'What an honour for me! You can spend the night here on the house!' 'Not *in* the house?' asked Obelix doubtfully. 'Won't it be rather chilly on the roof?' 'He means we can stay in the house on the house – free,' said Asterix. 'Thanks, Beeswax!' *Go to 42.*

27

As they had to guess at the seaport where troops had been landing, the Gauls thought perhaps it might be worth going to Dubris, on the off-chance. But as they stood discussing their next move, a Roman soldier suddenly walked out of one of the houses. 'Hey!' he told the British villager. 'Those are Gauls!' 'Yes, they're harmless Gaulish tourists, noble sir,' the villager told him. 'If those two are harmless Gaulish tourists, I'll eat my helmet!' said the Roman. 'They're the notorious Asterix and Obelix, they are, and they're known to have left Gaul on an undercover mission to Britain. Seize them, and Caesar will be eternally grateful to you!' 'That's torn it,' muttered Asterix, swallowing some magic potion, and, fighting their way out of the Romano-British village, he and Obelix set off as fast as they could go up the road to the camp of Delphinium, which would lead them back to Anticlimax's village.

Remove a *MAGIC POTION CARD* from *ASTERIX'S WAIST-SLIT*. Now go to 160.

'I'm afraid we haven't any money, or we'd willingly pay you compensation,' said Asterix. He thought for a moment. 'It really is a shame about your front door – but I know what we can do about it. Not much good at carpentry, are you, Obelix?' 'No,' said Obelix, catching his drift, 'but I can pick you a nice tree if you like.' And he marched off into a nearby wood, uprooted a vast oak and came back with it, while Asterix downed some magic potion, borrowed carpenter's tools from the Briton, and then set to work. In a few minutes, before the Briton's astonished eyes, he had made a brand-new front door and hung it in place. 'Well, I never did!' said the ancient Briton, his jaw dropping. 'No, of course you didn't. It takes magic potion to do that,' Obelix explained. Much impressed, the Briton told them the way to the village, and where they could spend the night in some hills called the Downs.

Remove a *MAGIC POTION CARD* from *ASTERIX'S WAIST-SLIT*. Now go to 149.

'*RAM* is correct!' said the decurion. 'Pass, friends, and all's well!' He seemed quite friendly, for a Roman, so Asterix chatted to him for a while and made sure they were on the right road. 'Yes,' said the decurion. 'Carry on along Watling Street, and you should reach Viroconium by nightfall.' Dogmatix, who had been stretching his legs, jumped back into the chariot just as they were starting off again, with something in his mouth. 'Hullo,' said Obelix, investigating, 'it's a bag of coins!' 'Oh dear,' said Asterix. 'I suppose we ought to turn round and take it back – he must have picked it up from the Romans at that roadblock!' But when they looked inside the bag, they found that the coins it contained were all Gaulish. 'That means they've been taken from Gaul as tax or tribute, so the Romans have no real right to them,' Asterix decided, and they drove on towards Viroconium.

If OBELIX is not already carrying the COINBAG, put it in his WAIST-SLIT. Now go to 38.

Once they had found out the right way to go from the butcher, who gave Dogmatix another bone, the Gauls went on, hoping to get as much of the journey behind them as they could before nightfall. Coming to a village, they found some little boys playing at sword-fighting in the street. 'Here, that's not the way to hold a sword!' said Asterix, laughing, as he showed one boy how to do it. Looking at the two Gauls, the children began to whisper. 'I say – you're not the famous Asterix and Obelix, are you?' one of them ventured to ask. 'That's us,' Asterix admitted. 'But we're on a secret mission, so mind you don't tell any Romans.' 'Wouldn't dream of it!' said the boy. 'Look – would this be useful? We . . . er . . . sort of borrowed it from a Roman tax-collector who came to the village!' Asterix thanked him for the password scroll he had produced, and said it would certainly come in useful. 'Perhaps you can tell us where we could spend the night?' he asked. 'Oh yes – my auntie keeps a bed and breakfast place! She'd be proud to have you to stay!' said the boy.

If OBELIX is not already carrying it, put the PASSWORD SCROLL in his WAIST-SLIT. Now go to 109.

31

Dogmatix was feeling full of beans. (He had had them for breakfast.) He scampered out into the street and up to a passing druid, tugging at the druid's robe until he walked over to speak to Asterix and Obelix. When they explained that they wanted to know the best route to Mona, the druid became very suspicious. 'Mona is a sacred island, and we druids guard our secrets closely!' he said. 'Do you know the password which would admit you to our druidical mysteries?'

Is OBELIX carrying a PASSWORD SCROLL? If so, find out the correct password by placing it exactly over the scroll shape on the next page, and follow the appropriate instruction. If not, you must guess which instruction to follow.

```
A    R    B    RE

DM   E   NO   I   E

L    LA   US    EI

LL      TE     SC

OLL      LI   GE

A       RC  H    I

T    Y   PT    EA

LO      B    O

T      O   ME
```

If you think it's MISTLETOE	go to 275
If you think it's PARSLEY	go to 97
If you think it's THYME	go to 84

32

'Durovernum is the nearest,' said Obelix, checking on the map. 'Oh yes!' said the ancient Briton. 'I remember hearing of your friends' village now! Little place in Cantium, isn't it? That's the way to go!' But as the Gauls started off in the direction to which he was pointing, he called them back. 'Wait a moment! I'm all for folk joining our brave boys who resist the Roman conquerors – I've got something here that might come in useful.' And he handed them a translator tablet. 'I found it in the flower-bed after a bunch of hefty great Romans marched over my lawn one day.' Asterix thanked the Briton, who asked if they would like to stay the night, but Asterix thought they'd better put part of the journey behind them before they stopped to rest. 'Well, you'll find a shepherd's hut up on the Downs,' said the ancient Briton. 'You could stop for the night there.'

If OBELIX is not already carrying it, put the TRANSLATOR in his WAIST-SLIT. Now go to 149.

33

Dogmatix saw an inn called the Chariot and Horses first. As a reward, Asterix and Obelix ordered him a huge pile of bones. But while they sat eating their own meal, they heard the landlord of the inn talking to a shifty-looking character in a language they couldn't understand. Both were casting glances at the Gauls on the sly. There was something about this that Asterix didn't quite like. 'I wish we could understand what those two are saying,' he whispered to Obelix. 'Do you have a translator on you?'

Is OBELIX carrying a TRANSLATOR? If so, use it to find out what the innkeeper is saying in the picture below and follow the instruction given. If not, go to 128.

34

Dogmatix was first to reach the mushrooms. He ate rather a lot, while the other two picked busily. All of a sudden they heard a harsh voice. 'Here, what do you think you're doing? This wood is now Roman property!' Looking up, the Gauls saw a Roman civilian looking sourly at them. 'I'm sorry,' said Asterix. 'We didn't know.' 'And you've been picking mushrooms too!' said the Roman. 'You'll have to pay for them – two coins, and hurry up about it!' 'What – pay for a few measly mushrooms?' said Obelix. 'I think we'd better, to save trouble,' said Asterix. 'That is, if we can!'

Is OBELIX carrying a COINBAG? If so, count out two coins by rotating the disc and go to the number shown on the other side. If not, go to 9.

35

'We're in luck,' said Asterix, interpreting. 'This chariot conductor is a patriotic Briton, and he's heard of us and our mission. He says the mistletoe has all been taken away to be locked up in the palace of Encyclopaedicus Britannicus, the Governor.' The chariot conductor said something else, and pressed the bag of coins which was his day's takings into Asterix's hands. 'And he's giving us this coinbag in case we need it for bribes!' Asterix said. 'Let's get off the chariot and go to the Governor's palace!'

If OBELIX is not already carrying the COINBAG, put it in his WAIST-SLIT. Now go to 2.

The Gauls paid their entrance fee, and the druid showed them all round Stonehenge. Asterix and Dogmatix were most impressed by the dolmens, although Obelix was rather more critical. 'You can't beat a good menhir, that's what I always say,' he remarked – but under his breath, so as not to sound rude. The friendly druid was pleased with their interest in his monument, and as it was almost dark by the time they had finished seeing round, he told them somewhere they could stay the night. 'It's a bed and breakfast place not far from here,' he said. ***Go to 109.***

'I say!' said Asterix, as they worked out what the Thracian sentry was saying. 'The big attack on the village is to take place tomorrow, when plenty of reinforcements have arrived! Quick! We must go straight back to the village!' Dogmatix, who had gone for a little run, rejoined them under the tree. He was carrying something in his mouth. 'Hullo, this looks like a map!' said Asterix. 'He must have found it lying around outside the camp somewhere. It should come in useful once we've helped defend the village and we start off after our mistletoe. Well done again, Dogmatix!'

If OBELIX is not already carrying the MAP, put it in his WAIST-SLIT. Now go to 211.

When they reached Viroconium, the Gauls were tired, and ready for a good night's rest, but they got up feeling ready for anything in the morning. 'I'm not at all sure how we'll find our way to Mona from here, though,' said Asterix. 'We'd better ask someone.'

Throw the special DICE to decide who asks the way to Mona.

If you throw ASTERIX	go to 224
If you throw OBELIX	go to 223
If you throw DOGMATIX	go to 31

'Glevum is wrong,' said Centurion Armisurplus. 'Well, you can't expect us to know the map of Britain off by heart,' protested Asterix. 'We're only here on holiday!' 'I know the sort of thing you Armorican Gauls get up to on holiday!' said Armisurplus. 'For all I know, you've come to supply the Britons with that magic potion your druid brews . . . what's that, at your belt?' 'This?' said Asterix, taking a gourd of magic potion from his belt and feeding it to Dogmatix. 'Only water! I mean, would I give it to the dog if it was magic potion?' Dogmatix supplied the answer to that by tearing into the legionaries, tossing them in the air – and by the time they had picked themselves up, he and the two Gauls were a long way up the road to the village. 'And here's a tablet with Armisurplus's orders – I picked it up in the general confusion!' said Asterix. 'It says the Romans are to prepare to attack the village tomorrow – that's just what we wanted to know!'

Remove a MAGIC POTION CARD from ASTERIX'S WAIST-SLIT. Now go to 211.

'It's Deva,' said Asterix, consulting the map. 'Then that's where we must go!' They were just setting off in their hired chariot when the landlord of the inn came running after them. 'Sorry I couldn't be more help,' he panted, 'but I thought this might come in useful.' And he handed them a password scroll. 'A Roman soldier who

stayed at my inn left it behind – you're welcome to it if you'd like it.'
'Thank you very much!' said Asterix. 'Deva, here we come!'

If OBELIX is not already carrying the PASSWORD SCROLL,
put it in his WAIST-SLIT. Now go to 153.

41

'Yes, I know we never have to pay for mushrooms picked in the
forest at home, Obelix,' Asterix whispered as he handed over the
money the Roman wanted, 'but we're going to need all our energies
for serious things like mistletoe! Let's not kick up a big fuss about
this. We didn't know we had to pay,' he said, turning to the
Roman. 'You see, we're foreigners, over to see the beautiful sights of
Britain under its Roman conquerors, so we had no idea of the local
customs. I suppose you're head forester in charge of all the woods in
Britain, are you? How well you look after them!' He guessed he was
flattering the Roman, who wasn't nearly important enough to be
head forester of all Britain, but it worked. 'Going to look around the
country, are you? Then you can have this – it'll help you understand
the natives!' said the official, producing a stone tablet with a list of
foreign words on it. 'See? Politeness pays, Obelix!' said Asterix just a
little smugly, as the two Gauls and Dogmatix walked away.

If OBELIX is not carrying the TRANSLATOR already, put it
into his WAIST-SLIT. Now go to 255.

After a good night's rest at the Queen Boadicea, Asterix and Obelix said goodbye to the landlord, Beeswax, and set out for the little village where Anticlimax, Chief Mykingdomforanos, and their friends lived. Beeswax showed them the main road out of Dubris. After a little while, however, they came to a signpost where three roads met. 'It says Rutupiae, Portus Lemanis, and Durovernum,' said Asterix, reading the wording on the signpost. 'I wonder which of them is closest to the village? If you've got a map on you, Obelix, we can look at it and decide which way to go.'

Is OBELIX carrying a MAP? If so, consult it to decide which of the three towns is closest to Anticlimax's village, and follow the appropriate instruction. If not, you must guess which instruction to follow.

If you think it's DUROVERNUM	go to 10
If you think it's PORTUS LEMANIS	go to 108
If you think it's RUTUPIAE	go to 44

'It's no good,' said Asterix. 'We'll just have to go on and hope for the best!' They were on their guard, however, as they set out from Bravoniacum, and weren't taken entirely by surprise when a troop of Roman soldiers jumped out at them. The legionaries had been watching the road north from the town. 'Oh no, you don't!' said Asterix, swallowing some magic potion and grabbing two legionaries in each hand. 'We're not going to be stopped now we're so near our goal!' As the Gauls drove off, they heard one of the flattened soldiers mutter to another, 'Just wait till they get to the Wall on the border! They'll change their tune then.' 'I doubt it,' said Asterix, 'but at least we know we're not far from the border of Caledonia.'

Remove a MAGIC POTION CARD from ASTERIX'S WAIST-SLIT. Now go to 123.

The Gauls went on along the road to Rutupiae. On the outskirts of the town, they decided that walking was thirsty work, and they would stop at the next inn they came to. 'If we can see a place with goats grazing, there's a chance we can get some goat's milk,' suggested Obelix. 'Look – there *is* a pub with a goat tethered in front of it!' This looked hopeful, and Asterix went in to order drinks while Obelix and Dogmatix stayed outside making friends with the goat. Inside, however, Asterix found the innkeeper arguing heatedly with a Roman official, who was waving a heavy stone tax slab in front of his face. 'Hullo,' said Asterix, 'what seems to be the trouble?' 'The trouble,' said the Roman 'is that Mr Nicknax here has not paid VAT on an imported vat of Gaulish wine.' 'I *have* paid VAT – you've just let the slab slip down the back of your desk or something!' said the innkeeper indignantly. 'You VATmen are getting my goat!' 'We are indeed!' agreed the official. 'I saw one grazing outside – we'll take it instead of payment.' Asterix decided to put a quick stop to the argument by drinking some magic potion and flinging the Roman out. The grateful innkeeper gave them goat's milk on the house, but told them they were going the wrong way for Anticlimax's village. 'However, you can take a short cut this way, over the fields,' he added, pointing out the right direction.

Remove a MAGIC POTION CARD from ASTERIX'S WAIST-SLIT. Now go to 209.

Dogmatix chased eagerly up to the sentry on duty at the barracks entrance, barking in a friendly way – and straight on into the camp! 'Well, I suppose that's as good a notion as any, but he won't be able to tell us any information he finds out!' said Asterix. 'Come on, we'd better rescue him.' Next moment, they saw a centurion coming to meet them. He was saying something in a language they couldn't understand. 'Have you got a translator handy, Obelix?' asked Asterix.

Is OBELIX carrying a TRANSLATOR? If so, use it to find out what the centurion is saying and follow the direction in the speech bubble below. If not, go to 179.

46

'Very well,' said Asterix. 'Give him the money, Obelix! *We're* not mercenary,' he told the soldier. 'Money means nothing to us so long as we can have the mistletoe!' And they went on into the cellar. *Go to 235.*

47

'No, you don't know the password,' said Fishcax, frowning. 'I wish I *could* trust you – but you obviously just said *PARSLEY* because I'm a fishmonger.' 'But I really *am* Anticlimax's cousin Asterix, from Gaul,' said Asterix. 'I've heard of Asterix all right, but how can

I be sure of what you say?' asked the fishmonger. 'Like this!' said Asterix, drinking one of his precious potions. 'You've heard of our magic potion, haven't you? Well, watch!' And with one hand he picked up a cart standing in the road, juggled with it a bit and then put it down again. 'Amazing! Yes, I believe you now,' said the fishmonger. 'Sorry if I seemed rather crabby, but one can't be too careful these days – all sorts of people keep trying to mussel in and winkle out information. Here's some fish for you – and a tip: try the Roman camp of Chrysanthemum for information about troop movements.'

Remove a _MAGIC POTION CARD_ from _ASTERIX'S WAIST-SLIT_. _Now go to 171_.

48

The ancient Briton accepted the money to pay for his front door, and became quite friendly. 'Your fat friend doesn't know his own strength, does he?' he said to Asterix. 'Fat?' growled Obelix, taking offence. 'Now look here, you . . .' 'He's not fat, you know!' said Asterix. 'Just nicely covered! Now, sir,' he added, 'we were wondering if you could tell us the way to that little village in Cantium where Chief Mykingdomforanos and Anticlimax are holding out against the Romans?' 'Mykingdomforanos and Anticlimax? Good chaps, both of 'em!' said the Briton cordially. 'Yes, I can tell you how to get there – that's the way,' he said, pointing down the road.

'If you want to stop for the night, you'll find a shepherd's hut up in those hills – they're called the Downs!' Obelix thought Downs was a pretty funny name for a range of hills, but before he could say anything tactless, Asterix thanked the Briton again and hurried him away. *Go to 149.*

49

Obelix had a bag of coins, and although paying Cassius Ceramix's debts was not the way they had planned to use it, Asterix gave Centurion Outrageous the money. It then occurred to him to wonder if the centurion was telling the whole truth. 'And we'd like a receipt, please!' he said. 'Hm . . . would you, though?' said Outrageous, in some confusion. Obviously Asterix had guessed right – Cassius Ceramix had not owed as much as nineteen coins. 'Tell you what,' said Centurion Outrageous, 'I'll give you this useful translator tablet, and we'll forget about receipts – how's that?' Asterix took the translator, and decided it would be wiser not to go on pretending he was a friend of Cassius Ceramix. 'Well, goodbye!' he said, and went on, to Obelix, 'Let's stroll round the outside of the barracks fence, shall we?'

If OBELIX is not already carrying the TRANSLATOR, put it in his WAIST-SLIT. Then go to 11.

The Gauls sat down on the banks of a little river to decide on their plan of action. 'It's lunch-time – I say we should have a good meal next!' said Obelix. 'Well, as good a meal as we can hope to get in Britain, which isn't saying much,' he added. 'You may have a point there,' agreed Asterix. 'I'm rather peckish myself. We'll be no use to anyone if we don't keep our strength up. Let's walk along this little road and see if we can find one of those British pubs that serve food as well as warm beer.'

Throw the special DICE to decide who sees an inn first.

If you throw ASTERIX	go to 77
If you throw OBELIX	go to 194
If you throw DOGMATIX	go to 33

'Well, here we go – off to Britain in a little jolly-boat!' said Asterix, looking round at the waters of the Mare Britannicum, later known as the English Channel. 'Though *you're* not looking very jolly, Obelix! What's up?' 'We've forgotten something,' said Obelix, gloomily. 'Provisions. We ought to have brought some. Remember what the Britons eat? Boiled boar with mint sauce, washed down with warm beer!' However, Asterix was unsympathetic. 'You'll just have to put up with it in the good of the cause,' he said. 'Now, which way shall we row? We can go north-east, which will take us straight out to sea and is the shortest way over, but it's also the usual route taken by Roman galleys crossing to Britain. Or we could avoid Roman shipping by turning north or south-east before we cross.' 'Who wants to avoid Roman shipping?' said Obelix. 'The more Romans the merrier! I say we go straight over!' 'Obelix,' said Asterix, patiently, 'this is not a pleasure trip! It's a mistletoe hunt – and if the Romans have got wind of our mission, they'll go all out to stop us. I suggest we turn north before rowing over, to throw any pursuers off the scent.' At the word 'scent' Dogmatix pointed his nose south-east and barked excitedly, as if he scented something interesting – obviously that way was *his* choice.

Throw the special DICE to decide whose choice to follow.

If you throw ASTERIX   go to 214
If you throw OBELIX   go to 7
If you throw DOGMATIX   go to 20

52

'*HADRIAN* is wrong – I knew you didn't know the password,' said the large man, nastily. 'And just what, I wonder, *is* your business in these parts? I think we'll hand you over to our Roman friends, and let *them* find out!' Bother – we can't do with this sort of delay, thought Asterix, swallowing a magic potion as he saw a number of Romano-British collaborators coming out into the street. 'Come along, Obelix – let's get out of here!' Which they did, leaving some very surprised and rather stunned collaborators behind them. 'This road leads to the camp of Delphinium, doesn't it?' said Asterix, as they left the Romano-British village behind them. 'We might as well take a look at it on our way back to Mykingdomforanos.'

Remove a *MAGIC POTION CARD* from *ASTERIX'S WAIST-SLIT*. Now go to 160.

53

Obelix paid for the sausages, the leg of boar and the pies. 'I think that's as much as we ought to carry, Obelix,' Asterix said. 'We're supposed to be travelling light, remember.' 'Obelix?' said the pork butcher, getting quite excited. 'Are you really the famous Obelix? And you must be Asterix! What an honour to have you in my shop!

I've heard of your heroic deeds in Britain. Where are you going?' He seemed a good sort of Briton, so Asterix told him. 'The best of luck!' said the butcher. 'Would you like this map of Britain? I've had it for ages, but I don't do much travelling. You're welcome to take it. Look – go *that* way,' he added, pointing to the map, 'and you'll come to a big crossroads. That's your best way to start out for Mona.'

If OBELIX is not already carrying the MAP, put it in his WAIST-SLIT. Now go to 107.

54

'Here you are!' said Asterix, giving the soldier the bribe he asked for. This was no time for argument. 'Come on, Obelix! Come on, Dogmatix!' he called, and they all ran down the cellar steps. There were two doors at the bottom, one on the right, one on the left. 'I wonder which leads to the cellar with the mistletoe in it?' said Asterix. 'Let's try this one on the right!' *Go to 201.*

55

'No, *CAESAR* is wrong,' said the centurion. 'Our old friend Julius wouldn't be very pleased to hear you say that, would he, when I was only being loyal?' said Asterix. 'Nonsense – you didn't know the password, and you're trying to wriggle out of it!' said the centurion. He and his men, hardened by their campaigning against the Picts and Scots along the Wall, looked a very tough lot indeed, and it was obvious they weren't easily going to let the Gauls by. Now if ever was a time for magic potion! Asterix drank some, and he and Obelix jumped down from the chariot, leaving Dogmatix to keep the horses in order by barking orders at them. The road was soon clear of Romans. 'Right!' said Asterix. 'We can go on to the Wall now!'

Remove a MAGIC POTION CARD from ASTERIX'S WAIST-SLIT. Then go to 123.

As Obelix had no map, they decided to ask Ekonomikrisis to drop them off at Portus Adurni. Obelix jumped back on board, and they sailed on towards the south coast of Britain, leaving the unfortunate Roman captain all at sea. *Go to 142.*

'Here you are,' said Asterix, handing over the money. 'You won't make many friends on the high seas this way, though!' 'We're not out to make friends,' said Timandahaf, with a sinister laugh. 'We're looking for countries to conquer! We thought of having a go at Britain – know anything about the place, do you?' 'Asterix, tell them to leave Britain alone!' Obelix begged in a whisper. 'We don't want these Normans pinching any of our Romans!' Asterix decided it was true that a Norman invasion might make Operation Britain even more complicated. 'Britain's still under the Roman Conquest,' he said. 'I'd wait a few centuries if I were you – you'd stand a better chance of a Norman Conquest then!' 'Thanks for the tip,' said Timandahaf. He was genuinely grateful – not grateful enough to give the Gauls their money back, but he gave them something in exchange. 'Here, we won't be needing this map of Britain now – you can have it!' he said, as the Gauls set off to row over the Mare Britannicum.

If OBELIX is not already carrying the MAP, put it in his WAIST-SLIT. Now go to 92.

Dogmatix rushed eagerly up to the British villager, barking and wagging his tail. However, the man didn't seem to like dogs; he only backed away. A woman coming out of her house bent to pat him on the head. But her large, ferocious-looking husband came out of the house too, behind her. 'You look like Gauls!' he said. 'We are,' Asterix told him, 'and we're . . .' Before he could start on their story of being Gaulish tourists out to see the sights of Roman Britain, however, the man said, 'Then you've got no right to come into this village without giving the password. It's a new Roman rule! Well – *can* you give it?'

Is OBELIX carrying a PASSWORD SCROLL? If so, find out the correct password by placing it exactly over the scroll shape below, and then follow the appropriate instruction. If not, you must guess which instruction to follow.

```
    B   RI    T      O

        C P        FS   A    Z

    !    L M       S   G

        W R E    6      7

  F   AL   S     E      T

         A   T    O      PPI

    D    U M  R      H    I

    C   H     A E       C

    A    H     O C    9!
```

If you think it's CAESAR	go to 14
If you think it's CLAUDIUS	go to 110
If you think it's HADRIAN	go to 52

'Yes,' said the villager, pocketing the money, 'I *have* seen Roman troops passing this way. They were making for the fortified camp of Delphinium. Don't ask me what for – that's all I know!' 'Rather a measly bit of information for the money,' said Asterix ruefully, as he, Obelix and Dogmatix left the Romano-British village. 'However, it might be a good idea to take a look a Delphinium as we pass it.' *Go to 160.*

They started off towards Durovernum . . . after a while, however, they realised that they had been to the place before, and it was not all that close to Londinium. It was bad luck that just as they had decided they ought to go another way, a Roman patrol came marching out of Durovernum. 'Here, you!' said the decurion in command. 'You two look like Gauls! And there's a "Wanted" notice out for two Gauls . . . I think you'd better come with us!' 'I don't!' said Asterix, taking some magic potion, and once the patrol was flattened, he, Obelix and Dogmatix set off across country.

Remove a MAGIC POTION CARD from ASTERIX'S WAIST-SLIT. Now go to 18.

'Since we haven't got a map, and Ekonomikrisis doesn't know the south coast of Britain well, we might try Isca,' said Asterix, as the Phoenician ship sailed away from Captain Nautilus and his galley, with Obelix back on board. Soon they were within sight of the British coast, and turned west. But as they went along, Asterix calculated their position by the sun, and decided they were going the wrong way for Anticlimax's village. 'Could you put us off as soon as possible?' he asked Ekonomikrisis. 'Right,' said the Phoenician. 'I think we're just coming to Portus Adurni.' *Go to 142.*

62

Luckily, they were able to pay the owner of the stables the thirteen coins he was asking. 'We're bound for the borders of Caledonia,' said Asterix, looking doubtfully at the countryside around them. There seemed to be a great deal of it, and nothing much in the way of landmarks to help them find their way. 'Can you tell us how we'll know when we actually get to the border?' 'Oh, that's easy,' said the man. 'The Romans have built a huge great Wall along the border, to keep the Picts and Scots from coming down south. You can't miss it. What do you want to go to Caledonia for, if you don't mind my asking?' Asterix hesitated for a moment, and then, as the man seemed friendly, told him part of their story. 'So you're on a mission from Gaul to the druids of Scotland?' said the owner of the stables. 'The Scottish druids tend to speak Gaelic – you may not be able to understand them. Here, have this translator tablet. It might help.'

If OBELIX is not already carrying the TRANSLATOR, put it in his WAIST-SLIT. Then go to 123.

63

'Now, we'd better think up some kind of story as an excuse for walking into this camp,' said Asterix, as they approached the fortified Roman camp of Obelix's choice – Delphinium. But as it turned out, even the best of stories would have been wasted on the sentry guarding the camp gates, who looked blankly at them as they politely asked permission to come in, and started chattering away in a foreign language. They couldn't make head or tail of what he was saying! 'He must be from one of the most distant Roman provinces,' said Asterix. 'Obelix, if you've got a translator tablet, we might find out what he's trying to tell us.'

Is OBELIX carrying a TRANSLATOR? If so, use it to find out what the sentry in the picture below is telling the Gauls to do. If not, go to 249.

64

Without a map, there was no way of telling which town was closest to the capital. 'I'm sure I've heard of Aquae Sulis,' said Asterix. 'Let's walk on to the nearest village and see if anyone there can help us.' But they had to ask a great many people before anyone knew about Aquae Sulis. 'Oh, that's miles away!' a villager told them at last. 'They've got some of those new-fangled Roman baths there. But I don't hold with all this bathing. It's not healthy.' 'I see – well, have you any idea where Eboracum and Verulamium are?' asked Asterix. 'Ah, well now, Verulamium isn't all that far away,' said the villager. 'Thanks – that's all we wanted to know!' Asterix told him. 'If the extra Roman troops are coming from Verulamium, we'd better go back to Anticlimax's village with our news,' he said to the others, as they hurried away. *Go to 211.*

As the corrupt Roman official was gleefully pocketing the money, he never noticed Dogmatix snatching something dangling from his belt. It was a scroll listing the passwords used all over the Roman Empire. Dogmatix raced away with it. Soon the Gauls were talking to Ekonomikrisis the Phoenician, who was surprised and pleased to see his old friends. 'As it happens, I'm going to Britain anyway,' he said. 'I can give you a lift.'

If OBELIX is not already carrying the PASSWORD SCROLL, put it in his WAIST-SLIT. Now go to 206.

Dogmatix was delighted to be the first to see a chariot-hire place. He led the two Gauls in, proudly wagging his tail, and was first to jump up into the chariot they hired too. It was drawn by two horses. They drove on along Watling Street, and after a while thought they had better make sure they were going the right way. Seeing a girl walking down the road, they stopped to ask her. However, it seemed that she couldn't speak any language they knew, though it was plain from the signs she was making that she would like to help them if she could. 'I think she's a foreign slave-girl, and obviously she'd be happy to sabotage the plans of her Roman captors,' said Asterix. 'But we can't understand her unless we have a translator.'

Is OBELIX carrying a TRANSLATOR? If so, use it to find out what the slave-girl is saying and go to the number given in the speech bubble. If not, go to 272.

Asterix turned the chariot towards Segedunum, and they drove on beside the Wall for a little way. They had not gone far when they saw a group of Roman soldiers leaning over the top of the Wall itself, jeering. 'Ho, ho! So you're the Gauls who came over to get supplies of mistletoe! Didn't know a spy back in Gaul overheard your plan, did you? Wouldn't you like to know where the mistletoe is now?' 'Yes!' said Asterix grimly, swallowing some magic potion. He didn't mind the silly jeering, but he did want whatever information the Romans could give, and as Obelix was not exactly cut out for wall-climbing, it was up to Asterix to go up there and thump the Romans into telling him where the mistletoe was. 'All taken to Londinium,' they gasped, 'and please stop hitting us!' 'Well, there's nothing for it,' said Asterix, climbing down. 'We must go back to Londinium!'

Remove a _MAGIC POTION CARD_ from _ASTERIX'S WAIST-SLIT. Now go to 115._ (Remember: when there are no magic potion cards left in Asterix's waist-slit Operation Britain cannot go on, and you must start the game again.)

Obelix cheerfully paid the fishmonger the money he asked. 'And cheap at the price!' he said. 'Those fish look lovely!' Fishcax seemed pleased – and then he looked more closely at Obelix. 'You're not Obelix the Gaul, are you?' he said. 'That's right, he is,' said Asterix, 'and I'm Asterix the Gaul, and this is Dogmatix the Gaulish dog!' 'It's a privilege to meet you!' said Fishcax. 'Now listen – I have some information you might like! There's something fishy going on at Chrysanthemum – here, take this! It's a password scroll we winkled out of headquarters in Londinium, and it could be useful to you. Take this fish too – no, of course I wouldn't dream of taking any money for it – and the best of British and Gaulish luck to all three of you!'

If OBELIX is not already carrying the PASSWORD SCROLL, put it in his WAIST-SLIT. Now go to 171.

Anderida was the closest of the three British towns to Anticlimax's village. 'Right, I'm leaving your ship now!' Obelix told Captain Nautilus. 'But first, how about some compensation for inconvenience to Ekonomikrisis in stopping his ship?' Feeling very shaken, Captain Nautilus handed over a bag of coins. Obelix offered it to Ekonomikrisis as they sailed on towards Anderida, but the grateful Phoenician told the Gauls to keep it.

If OBELIX isn't already carrying the COINBAG, put it in his WAIST-SLIT. Now go to 132.

'*WINE!*' guessed Asterix. 'No, it isn't,' said the man who had challenged them. Some more Iceni, armed with spears, came up behind him. 'I'm sorry, but we can't help not knowing your password!' said Asterix. 'We wouldn't want to hurt you, so will you let us pass all the same?' 'Wouldn't want to hurt us – what, you two and a dog?' guffawed the Briton. 'That's a good joke, that is!' 'Oh no, it isn't!' said another of the Iceni, suddenly. 'I know who these men are – haven't you ever heard of Asterix and Obelix, from Armorica? You *are* Asterix and Obelix, aren't you?' 'That's right,' said Asterix. 'We're on a very important mission to Britain. Look, have you heard of our magic potion too?' The man who knew their names nodded. 'Well, let us pass and we'll give you this gourd full of it!' said Asterix, offering him one. 'That's a very handsome offer,' said the man. 'In return, I'm sure Queen Boadicea will be happy to give you any advice she can. If you'd like to come into the fort, you can meet her.'

Remove a *MAGIC POTION CARD* from *ASTERIX'S WAIST-SLIT*. *Now go to 200.*

71

They paid the three coins, and went on over Londinium Bridge. 'Now, if the mistletoe is *not* in the Tower, what do you think *is* the most likely place for it?' said Asterix, thoughtfully, and answered his own question. 'The Governor's palace! I'm sure Encyclopaedicus Britannicus wants to keep an eye on it himself, or he'd have stored it in the high-security Tower. So let's go to his palace!' *Go to 2.*

Reaching Durovernum, the Gauls stopped to talk to a friendly passer-by. 'From Gaul, are you?' he said. 'I'd go and see the Arch-Druid of Durovernum if I were you. I'm sure he'd put you up for the night in his palace.' 'A palace sounds rather too grand for us,' said Obelix. 'Oh, that's just what they call an Arch-Druid's house,' said the Briton. The Arch-Druid himself listened sympathetically to the tale of the Gauls' mission, and told them he and Getafix had often met at the Druid of the Year contests in the Forest of the Carnutes. 'Of course you can stay the night,' he said. 'I only wish I could do more to help – but we druids are not very popular with the Roman invaders.' Next morning, he told them how to reach Anticlimax's village, and they set off. There were two Roman soldiers on guard at the gates of the town, busy talking to each other. 'I wonder what they're saying?' said Asterix. 'Let's sit down on this bench by the gate, pretend to be admiring the view, and listen!' However, the Roman soldiers were mercenaries from Thrace, and the Gauls couldn't understand what they said without a translator.

Is OBELIX carrying a TRANSLATOR? If so, use it to find out what the soldiers are saying in the picture below, and follow the instruction given. If not, go to 4.

73

The Gauls paid up, went into the Briton's house, and sat down to a not very appetising meal. 'This is a bit of a bore,' grumbled Obelix, poking at the greyish meat on his plate, 'and not a very big bit, either.' 'It'll keep us going, even if it isn't up to the usual standards of British hospitality – I'm sure you'll get plenty to eat when we reach Anticlimax's village.' 'They're hospitable enough, but they boil everything there, too,' Obelix reminded his friend. 'I bet they've even taken to stewing their tea by now!' 'Oh, do stop making such a fuss!' said Asterix, and they ate up their meal and prepared to continue their journey. Asterix felt it would be better not to mention the little village in Cantium – there was something he didn't quite trust about the look of their host – so he just asked the way to Durovernum, which he knew was in the right direction. *Go to 72.*

74

'Now, you watch *me* bluff!' said Obelix, walking up to the sentry at the entrance to the barracks. 'Hi there!' he said. 'How about giving us a spot of military information?' The astonished sentry just gaped at him. 'Inf . . . information?' he said, completely at a loss. 'Er . . . er . . . well, what's the password, then?'

Is OBELIX carrying a PASSWORD SCROLL? If so, use it to find out the correct password by placing it exactly over the scroll

*shape below. **Then follow the appropriate instruction. If he
doesn't have one, you'll have to guess which instruction to
follow.***

BA   U   D   ET

L   AIS   R   E

R   I   M T   BA

UD   V ER   L

A I   N

EG   US   T

A   V   G F   L

AU   B E   R

S   T   RA   N

If you think it's GOAT	go to 282
If you think it's RAM	go to 91
If you think it's STAG	go to 22

75

Captain Nautilus scowled. 'No, *THYME* is wrong,' he said.
'You're just guessing. I think we'll take you and your friend there
into custody while we investigate! And the Phoenician captain too –
you there, Phoenician, I'm confiscating your cargo!' But this was
too much for Ekonomikrisis; the mere idea of losing his precious
property made him brave enough to stand up to any threats. 'Oh no,
you're not! Men, start rowing!' he bellowed, and before the Roman
captain realised what they were about, all the oarsmen suddenly

swept the vessel on and out of reach of the larger, slower galley, making for the British port of Anderida. ***Go to 132.***

76

Obelix gave the peasant his eight coins, and the man apologised for having to ask for payment. 'I'm a true-blue Briton,' he explained. 'That's why I wear this woad. But I've a wife and children to keep, and the Roman taxes have beggared me. You wanted to know about Boadicea? She led a successful revolt, somewhere to the north-east of Londinium . . . and Governor Encyclopaedicus Britannicus wasn't best pleased. I'm afraid that's about all I can tell you.' 'It's interesting, though,' said Asterix thoughtfully. 'Tell you what,' said the man, 'you might find out more if you went to one of the fortified Roman camps.' 'Good idea,' agreed Asterix. 'I should think Antirrhinum's the nearest to here, isn't it?' 'That's right,' said the peasant, 'and look – here's something you might be able to use! I sort of . . . er, borrowed this tablet full of foreign words from the local tax collector, but it's not done me much good.'

If OBELIX is not already carrying the TRANSLATOR, put it in his WAIST-SLIT. Then go to 192.

77

Asterix was the first to see a pub with a sign saying it was the Chariot and Horses. The Gauls went in and sat down to order a meal. But the landlord, a rather sour-faced man, seemed strangely reluctant to serve them. From the way he was talking, Asterix soon realised that he was one of those Britons who collaborated with the Roman conquerors. 'I hope you're loyal to our wonderful Roman rulers,' said the landlord. 'I don't serve meals to just anyone, you know!' 'Then you must find it rather hard to make ends meet,' said Asterix. 'Speaking of meat, can you do a nice roast boar, rare?' asked Obelix hopefully. 'I mean cooked rare – though Toutatis knows roast boar's rare enough in this country.' 'I'll want you to prove your credentials before I serve you,' the innkeeper went on. 'Can you give the password for this part of Britain?'

Is OBELIX carrying a PASSWORD SCROLL? If so, find the correct password by placing it exactly over the scroll shape below. Then follow the appropriate instruction. If not, you will have to guess which instruction to follow.

```
   O  T  B   L        A
  C    KB  H    I    LL
  I     AR   Y        D
   CE     RE     B
  AL     LM    S     G
   W     RL      NE
  R    SR  I  E   LA
  N   K   A    S    ER
   E   N D    I     PI
```

If you think it's MISTLETOE   go to 105
If you think it's PARSLEY   go to 169
If you think it's THYME   go to 198

Relieved to find they could pay the bill for their dinner, Asterix counted out the money. 'Do you know the quickest way to get to Caledonia?' he asked the steak-house manager. 'Straight on up the Fosse Way to Lindum,' said the man. *Go to 180.*

As the Gauls were about to open the left-hand cellar door – with one of Obelix's gentle little taps if necessary – a Roman legionary came out of it. They could see mistletoe inside. 'Lots of lovely mistletoe!' breathed Asterix. The legionary recognised the Gauls at once – 'Wanted' slabs, showing their pictures, had just arrived from Gaul to help the Romans in Britain track them down. Fighting them was obviously hopeless, but he was good at turning things to his own advantage. 'Ssh!' he said, putting a finger to his lips. 'I won't give you away, if you pay me twelve coins!'

Is OBELIX carrying a COINBAG? If so, count out twelve coins by rotating the disc, and go to the number shown on the other side. If not, go to 136.

'The password's not *MISTLETOE*,' said the guard. 'Well, that would be too easy, wouldn't it?' And just at that moment, Encyclopaedicus Britannicus, the Governor himself, appeared in the doorway behind the soldiers. 'It's the Gauls from Armorica!' he exclaimed. 'Quick, seize them!' *Go to 218.*

'What, charge us just to go down to the quayside?' said Obelix indignantly. 'This is a free country, isn't it?' 'No,' the official pointed out. 'It's occupied by the mighty Roman Empire, and might is right!' 'So it is!' said Obelix, knocking the Roman sky-high. 'Come on, you two! I can see Ekonomikrisis waving to us!' he added, and they all hurried down to the quay for a reunion with their friend. 'Of course I'll take you to Britain – sale or return,' he promised. 'Sail will do, we'll see about our own return,' said Asterix. **Go to 206.**

'You mean there's no reduction for dogs?' said Asterix. 'None at all,' said the toll-collector, taking their money. 'All right, you can go on up the road to Chrysanthemum now – oh, but you can't go inside, by the way! It's not open to the public.' 'You mean you've taken our money just to let us walk a few hundred metres up this road? Well, really, I call that a bit steep!' grumbled Obelix. 'Steep? It hardly slopes at all!' said the toll-collector, but the Gauls had moved out of earshot, still feeling indignant at being tricked into paying a toll for nothing. 'Well, no sense in crying over spilt milk,' said Asterix. 'Spilt milk? Where? I don't see any,' said Obelix, looking round. 'I mean our money,' Asterix explained. 'We must just sit down and plan our next move.' **Go to 50.**

'Well, well!' said Asterix, as the Gauls strolled away, looking as if they hadn't been eavesdropping at all. 'So those two legionaries were discussing a raid to be made on Anticlimax's village in the near future! What a good thing we overheard them – now we can warn the villagers to be prepared.' 'And here's another good thing,' said Obelix, producing a map. 'I found it under the bench where we were sitting. The Roman soldiers must have dropped it.' 'Well done, Obelix!' said his friend. 'That's sure to come in useful on our mistletoe mission. But we'll lend our British friends a hand first. Come on – I can't wait to see them all again!'

If OBELIX is not already carrying the MAP, put it into his WAIST-SLIT. Now go to 209.

84

'*THYME?*' Asterix wondered, but the druid told him that was not the password. He turned to walk away and leave the Gauls. 'Oh, do wait a moment!' said Asterix. 'Listen – have you heard of the Gaulish druid Getafix?' 'Of course!' said the druid. 'All druids have heard of Getafix, three times winner of the Druid of the Year contest in the Forest of the Carnutes!' 'Well, he's sent you this gourd of magic potion as a special present!' said Asterix, and explained their mission. The druid looked first astonished, and then very pleased when he opened the magic potion and sniffed at it. 'That's certainly a drop of the right stuff!' he said. 'You must be genuine after all! Go to Deva, and you'll find the druids there will help you on your way to Mona.'

Remove a MAGIC POTION CARD from ASTERIX'S WAIST-SLIT. Now go to 153.

85

'He's obviously a nasty, grasping character,' said Asterix, 'but we're in a hurry, so I suppose we'd better pay up.' Obelix gave the man his money, and got the information they wanted in exchange. 'You'll have to go on to Deva,' said the man, 'and from Deva you go round the coastline to Segontium, to avoid crossing the mountains. From Segontium, you can cross to Mona.' 'Good!' said Asterix. 'Let's go!' *Go to 153.*

86

'We want to make for Lindum!' said Asterix, consulting the map. 'It's north of here, on a road called the Fosse Way.' They hired a change of horses for the chariot Queen Boadicea had lent them, and soon they were driving northwards. *Go to 180.*

87

'He says Dogmatix is a nice little dog, but we can't bring him in here,' Obelix translated. 'However, we can give him a run outside the barracks fence if we like.' 'Oh well, I suppose that's better than nothing,' said Asterix. 'Here, Dogmatix!' And he whistled Dogmatix back to them, as they set off to walk round the outside of the perimeter fence. *Go to 11.*

They set off along the path leading away from the banks of the river Tamesis, and came to a place where three roads met, with a signpost pointing down them. Peering at it in the fading light, the Gauls saw that the three roads went to Londinium, Durovernum and Durobrivae. 'Now, I wonder which of those is on the way to that little village in Cantium . . . have you got a map there, Obelix?' asked Asterix.

Is OBELIX carrying a MAP? If so, consult it to see which town is nearest to Anticlimax's village and follow the appropriate instruction. If not, you must guess which instruction to follow.

If you think it's DUROBRIVAE   go to 95
If you think it's DUROVERNUM   go to 93
If you think it's LONDINIUM   go to 141

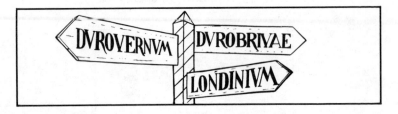

'So that innkeeper had recognised us and was planning to give us away – and the man he was talking to was a spy working for the Romans!' said Asterix. 'What a good thing we overheard and managed to get out of the Chariot and Horses while they were still talking!' 'Leaving half our meal behind us!' said Obelix, mournfully. 'Oh, come on, Obelix, you know you didn't think much of that boiled boar,' said Asterix. 'And at least Dogmatix has managed to bring one of his bones away with him.' *Go to 18.*

They rowed towards Anderida, but as they were coming in to the port, they saw a Roman galley heading the same way. 'Romans at last!' said Obelix, bouncing up and down in the jolly-boat with excitement. 'Obelix, please don't rock the boat!' said Asterix. 'We want to *avoid* the Romans if possible and make straight for the magic mistletoe, remember?' 'Never any fun,' said Obelix, gloomily. 'I'm going to sulk, so there, and serve you right!' But in spite of his sulks, he pulled on the oars to turn the boat and head for Dubris instead. *Go to 172.*

'I knew you wouldn't know!' said the sentry. 'No, the password's not *RAM*. So get out, before I ram you in the stomach with my spear! Looks a nice, big, bouncy stomach, just right for a bit of a shove with a spear,' he added. Seeing his friend about to thump the centurion for these insulting remarks, Asterix was going to stop him – but at that moment a number of legionaries came marching up along a side road, cutting him off from Obelix. He had to drink some magic potion in order to pass them and drag Obelix off the sentry. They both rejoined Dogmatix. 'Oh, yes, a brilliant bit of bluff that was!' said Asterix, sarcastically. 'Come on, we might at least look round the outside of this barracks, even if this sentry won't let us see inside.'

Remove a MAGIC POTION CARD from ASTERIX'S WAIST-SLIT. Now go to 11.

Eventually the Gauls found themselves rowing up the mouth of a river. 'This must be the Tamesis – the big river that flows through Londinium,' said Asterix, as he and Obelix pulled their boat up on land. 'Why don't we carry straight on upstream and pick up our mistletoe from the oak-wood near Londinium?' said Obelix. 'No, it would be wiser to go and see Anticlimax and his friends first,' said Asterix. 'They'll tell us the lie of the land!' 'Will they really? I always thought they were rather a truthful bunch,' said Obelix, surprised. 'I mean, they can tell us what's going on in Britain at the moment,' Asterix explained. 'Who knows what dangers await us? Now, I suggest we move on towards the village, under cover of dark.' '*I* suggest we find a meal,' said Obelix. Dogmatix, yapping hopefully, made it clear that after sitting still in a boat for so long, *he* wanted to run around and chase things. 'Menhirs – or rabbits, anyway,' said Obelix. 'I suppose he might catch us some supper.'

Throw the special DICE to decide what the Gauls do next.

If you throw ASTERIX	go to 88
If you throw OBELIX	go to 187
If you throw DOGMATIX	go to 273

The Gauls were in luck . . . not long after they started walking down the road to Durovernum, a Briton driving a cart full of barrels stopped and offered them a lift. 'What's in those barrels?' asked Obelix, interested. On hearing that it was warm beer, he almost refused the lift, but Asterix told him not to be silly; no one was actually asking them to drink the stuff. As they drove along, the carter filled them in on modern British history. 'They say Queen Boadicea has led a revolt of her tribe, the Iceni, against the Romans,' he said. 'Yes, the Romans are having a tough time hanging on to their conquest of these islands – up north, they've had to build a great big Wall to keep Chief McAnix and his Picts and Scots out. Well, here we are in the town – didn't you say your local druid had sent you here? Why not go and see the Arch-Druid of Durovernum?' *Go to 72.*

94

Dogmatix raced up to the sentries on duty at the gate of the Tower of Londinium, wagging his tail – but almost at once he ran back to Asterix and Obelix, shaking his head so hard that his floppy ears flew about. 'He's trying to tell us we'd be wasting our time in there,' said Obelix, who knew his dog very well. 'Hm . . . he's a clever dog, and he knows we're looking for mistletoe, so that means his nose tells him there's none in the Tower,' said Asterix. 'Let's go on over Londinium Bridge and into the city, then.' However, before they could cross the bridge, they were asked to pay a toll. 'That'll be three coins – one each, including the dog,' said the collector.

Is OBELIX carrying a COINBAG? If so, count out three coins by rotating the disc, and then go to the number shown on the other side. If not, go to 283.

95

The road to Durobrivae was fairly free of Roman soldiers, and the Gauls enjoyed a chance to stretch their legs – so did Dogmatix. Before too long they reached the town, and asked a woman the way to Anticlimax's village. 'What – the little village where Chief Mykingdomforanos and his men are still holding out against the invaders?' she said. 'Oh dear, I'm afraid you've come the wrong way. It's because the two town names sound rather like each other, I expect. You want to go to Durovernum, not Durobrivae!' But the Gauls did not have to retrace their steps to the signpost; the woman told them a short cut to Durovernum. ***Go to 72.***

96

'No, *CAESAR* is not the password!' said the decurion, looking at the Gauls more suspiciously than ever, and noticing Dogmatix for the first time. 'Two dangerous Gauls and a savage hound, that's what we're looking out for!' he added, meaningly. It was a pity Dogmatix chose this particular moment to get up on his hind legs and bark furiously at the Romans. 'Oh, bother!' said Asterix to himself. 'I'll just have to use up one of my gourds of magic potion.' Which he did, with results which surprised the men at the roadblock very much indeed. A few minutes later he was strolling up the road on the other side of it, whistling, with Obelix and Dogmatix. 'And now to find somewhere to spend the night,' he said.

Remove a MAGIC POTION CARD from ASTERIX'S WAIST-SLIT. Now go to 109.

97

The druid looked even more suspicious when Asterix said, 'Is it *PARSLEY*?' 'No!' he said. 'You were just guessing!' 'Well, in a way,' Asterix admitted. 'But if you'll listen to our story, you'll see why mistletoe means so much to us!' And he briefly told the druid all about Operation Britain. 'That's as may be,' said the druid. 'Of course I've heard of the famous Getafix – but how do I know you're really Asterix and Obelix?' 'I suppose you've heard of Getafix's potion?' said Asterix, swallowing some. 'Watch this!' And he picked up a dolmen which stood at one end of the street, carried it to the other end and put it down again. 'I believe you now!' said the druid, shaking hands and wishing them luck. 'The next stage on your journey to Mona should be to go to the town of Deva.' Within a few minutes, Asterix and Obelix were off.

*Remove a **MAGIC POTION CARD** from **ASTERIX'S WAIST-SLIT**. Now go to 153.*

98

Obelix got his way about the tartan trousers. 'And I've heard of something called haggis that the Caledonians make out of parts of a sheep,' he said, as the Operation Britain party set off for Caledonia. 'If I got the recipe, we could use it for boar.' It was going to be a long journey, but they were lucky enough to get a lift in a cart. The carter dropped them off, north-west of Londinium, and they walked on past Verulamium on foot. 'I wonder if we're going the right way?' said Asterix, after a while. 'We'd better ask the next person we meet.' Half an hour later, they did meet someone walking down the road towards them – he looked like a merchant. The trouble was, he was a foreign merchant, and could neither understand nor answer their question, though he seemed to be quite anxious to tell them something or other, from the way he kept talking excitedly and pointing up the road. 'What nationality *is* he, do you think?' Obelix asked. 'I'm not sure,' said Asterix. 'Something Mediterranean, I'd say – perhaps Greek, from the sound of what he's saying.' 'It's all Greek to me,' said Obelix, gloomily. 'If you've got a translator, Obelix, it might not be Greek to us even if it *is* Greek to us, if you see what I mean,' said Asterix. Obelix didn't, but he searched his pockets.

Is OBELIX carrying a TRANSLATOR? If so, use it to find out what the foreign merchant is saying, and follow the instruction given in the speech bubble below. If not, go to 16.

99

Asterix saw a chariot-hire place first. They went in, hired a chariot and pair, and checked that they were going in the right direction. 'Yes, keep on west,' said the man who was harnessing up the horses for them. 'You'll find it's easy enough driving along Watling Street – one thing I will say for the Romans, they build a good road.' Some way along the good road, however, it turned out that the Romans had also set up a good roadblock, and the Gauls came up against it. 'No way through unless you can give the password!' said the decurion in command.

*Is **OBELIX** carrying a **PASSWORD SCROLL**? If so, find the correct password by placing it exactly over the scroll shape below, and then follow the appropriate instruction. If not, you must guess which instruction to follow.*

```
   A    BE  L      I
   E     R   M        O
  U R   TO     NA  C
   IN    Q     P A
  TT    EA    S      F
  E     RN   AN     D
       E L P      IN
  O C C M     I     O
  E E       Y A     Y
```

If you think it's GOAT	go to 216
If you think it's RAM	go to 29
If you think it's STAG	go to 219

The ancient Briton had pointed vaguely eastward for Portus Lemanis, and realising that when they landed at Anderida, they were farther to the south and the west than when they had arrived in Britain before, Asterix decided it would be best to go east. So they went on until it began to get dark – and in the last of the evening light, they suddenly saw Portus Lemanis lying ahead, and the sea beyond it. 'I don't think this was quite right after all,' said Asterix. 'I know Anticlimax's village is inland, not by the seaside. But still, we can't have come too far out of our way. Let's strike up into those hills and see if we can find shelter for the night.' ***Go to 149.***

'Sorry, *STAG* is wrong,' said the centurion, but Dogmatix was frisking around his legs in a very friendly way – the clever little dog had realised that this Roman really liked dogs, and sure enough, the centurion bent down to pat him. 'Nice little chap, isn't he?' he said. 'Well, we'll forget about the password this time – but mind you get permission if you want to walk him after dark another time. Off you go, now!' Dogmatix obeyed him, chasing away down the path, and the Gauls followed. 'Better take the road to Durovernum!' the helpful centurion shouted after them. ***Go to 72.***

They went on along the road Obelix had chosen, and after a while they came to a sign saying STONEHENGE. 'Stonehenge!' said

Obelix, thrilled. 'I knew this was the road to take!' 'But Stonehenge is nowhere near Anticlimax's village,' Asterix objected. However, he hadn't the heart to deprive his menhir-loving friend of a chance to see the standing stones of Britain, so they went on to Stonehenge, and found a druid sitting by the entrance, with tickets. 'We don't have to pay, do we?' asked Asterix. 'Only seven coins for the three of you,' said the druid. 'There's a reduction for the dog, and it all goes to the upkeep of the ancient monument.' 'Fair enough,' said Asterix, 'but can we afford it? Have you got a bag of coins, Obelix?'

Is OBELIX carrying a COINBAG? If so, count out the seven coins by rotating the disc, and then go to the number shown on the opposite side. If not, go to 233.

103

'Right, let's try the Queen Boadicea!' said Asterix. 'It must be called after the Queen of the Iceni – I've heard my cousin Anticlimax mention her.' The inn looked very comfortable, and to Obelix's delight, there was real roast boar on the menu. (The landlord had once been on a day-trip to Portus Itius, which gave him a taste for Gaulish cuisine.) 'Can we afford it, though?' Asterix wondered, looking at the prices. He worked out that the bill would come to eighteen coins for the three of them. 'How much have we got, Obelix?' he asked his friend.

Is OBELIX carrying a COINBAG? If so, count out the eighteen coins by rotating the disc, and then go to the number that shows on the other side. If not, go to 234.

'No, the password's not *MEAD*,' said one of the sentries. 'We'd like to come in, all the same,' said Asterix. 'I dare say!' said the legionary, laughing a lot. 'And we will, if we want to,' said Obelix, 'so there!' 'Have you by any chance heard of the time some Gauls visited this Tower before?' asked Asterix. 'I've an idea I know your faces – weren't you on sentry duty then?' The sentries stopped laughing. 'Mucus, it's them!' one said to the other, in a terrified whisper. 'Porus, so it is!' his friend whispered back. 'The two indomitable Gauls – they're said to be looking for the magic mistletoe!' 'Exactly – so tell us where it is and be quick about it, will you?' said Asterix. 'The centurion will murder us if we do!' quavered Porus. 'And we'll murder you if you don't!' said Obelix, cheerfully. 'You know, it really *is* bad luck on them to be on sentry duty again this time,' said Asterix. 'Look, you two, I'll give you this gourd of magic potion – that will protect you from the wrath of your superior officers all right! Now tell us where the mistletoe is!' Thankfully, the legionaries accepted the potion, and told the Gauls that the mistletoe was all in the Governor's palace. They set off for the palace at once.

**Remove a *MAGIC POTION CARD* from *ASTERIX'S WAIST-SLIT. Now go to 2.* (Remember: when there are no magic potion cards left in Asterix's waist-slit Operation Britain cannot go on, and you must start the game again.)

'No, *MISTLETOE* is not the password!' said the innkeeper, looking positively pleased that the Gauls had guessed wrong. 'So I can't serve you!' 'Well, really, I'm not sure we'd *want* a meal served in that kind of spirit,' said Asterix, getting up to leave. 'I don't mind what kind of spirit it's served in – Gaulish brandy, Caledonian whisky, anything so long as it's not warm beer, though I'd rather have a boar simmered in goat's milk, if you really can't roast it,' said Obelix hopefully. He was bent on having his meal. 'Come on, Asterix – I'm ravenous! Let's see what we can find in the kitchen.' And he had gone off to explore before Asterix could stop him. The innkeeper was a large man – much bigger than Asterix, who had to take a quick drink of his precious magic potion to fend him off, go after Obelix, haul him out of the inn and away again.

Remove a *MAGIC POTION CARD* from *ASTERIX'S WAIST-SLIT*. Now go to 228.

106

'*CLAUDIUS* is not the password. You're coming back to Londinium with us for questioning,' said the centurion. 'Men, seize those Gauls!' 'Obelix,' Asterix whispered, 'you hold the reins while I lean over to the horses' heads, and then be ready to drive on!' Bending forward, he tipped half a gourd of magic potion into each horse's mouth. The horses had never tasted anything like it! When Obelix gave a great yell of 'Gee up there!' they galloped forward at tremendous speed, sending Romans flying in all directions, and soon they were trotting up the road again.

Remove a MAGIC POTION CARD from ASTERIX'S WAIST-SLIT. Now go to 123.

107

At the crossroads, a sign pointing down one of the two main Roman roads said ICKNIELD WAY. The other said WATLING STREET. 'It's Watling Street we want, if we're going over west towards the island of Mona,' said Asterix. 'And Mona's a long way off – I think we'd better hire a chariot. Let's see who can spot a place to hire one first.'

Throw the special DICE to decide who sees a chariot-hire place first.

If you throw ASTERIX	go to 99
If you throw OBELIX	go to 208
If you throw DOGMATIX	go to 66

108

They decided to take a chance on the road to Portus Lemanis – after a while, however, they decided it must have been the wrong choice. 'This road keeps giving us glimpses of the sea, which means we're following the coastline, and that can't be right,' said Asterix, frowning. 'I know the village isn't by the seaside. I suggest we go back. Let's try the Durovernum road this time.' And after they had gone some way towards Durovernum, the landscape began to look familiar. 'I think we'll reach the village quite soon now,' said Asterix. ***Go to 209.***

109

After a good night's rest in the bed and breakfast place they had found on the road going east towards Cantium, the two Gauls said goodbye to their hostess, who had provided an excellent breakfast of eggs, bacon and mushrooms – the British breakfast was one kind of British cooking Obelix *did* approve of. Soon they came to a place where three roads met. Looking at the signpost, they saw that these roads led to Venta Belgarum, Corinium and Lindinis. 'I've no idea which we ought to take to get to Cantium and Cousin Anticlimax's village,' said Asterix. 'Have you got a map so I can see where we are, Obelix?'

Is OBELIX carrying a MAP? If so, consult it to see which town is on the Gauls' way to Anticlimax's village, and follow the appropriate direction. If not, you must guess which direction to follow.

If you think it's CORINIUM	go to 197
If you think it's LINDINIS	go to 242
If you think it's VENTA BELGARUM	go to 23

110

'Ah, so you don't know the password! No, *CLAUDIUS* was the wrong guess!' said the man. And he aimed a kick at Dogmatix for no reason at all, and went into his house. 'Oh dear!' said his wife. 'Is your dear little dog all right?' 'Yes,' said Asterix, checking. And as the woman seemed friendly, he added, 'I suppose you can't tell us if there have been any Roman troops passing this way?' 'I could – but I'm frightened to,' said the poor woman. 'My husband wouldn't like it. He'd hit me if he knew.' 'Would he, though?' said Asterix, and on impulse he took out one of his gourds of magic potion and gave it to her. 'Next time he tries that, you drink a few drops of this potion, and you'll find the effect is quite surprising. So will he!' 'I'll tell you anyway,' said the woman. 'Yes, there have been troops passing by on their way to Delphinium!' 'Come on, Obelix – let's go back to Delphinium,' said Asterix, as they left the village.

Remove a MAGIC POTION CARD from ASTERIX'S WAIST-SLIT. Now go to 160.

111

'Yes, *GOAT* is right. Very well, you're allowed to walk the dog, then,' agreed the centurion. 'All these Roman rules and regulations get *my* goat,' muttered Obelix under his breath. 'But you're Gauls, aren't you?' went on the centurion. 'I've been stationed in Gaul – I recognise the accent! What are you doing over here?' 'Well, we know how our own country of Gaul has benefited from the Roman Conquest,' said Asterix, cheerfully making up this story as he went along, 'and we thought we'd like to see Britain, because we heard Britain was full of wonderful ruins too, now it's been conquered by the Romans. We're on a sight-seeing trip.' 'Fair enough,' said the centurion. 'You're right about the ruins! Here – you can have this map if you like, to help you find your way around the country. But now you'd better be off and get indoors till dawn. Your nearest town is Durovernum – that's the way!' He pointed it out, and the Gauls hurried off, chuckling at the success of their story. ***Go to 72.***

112

'He's telling us that we won't find any treasure down in the cellars, because the place is stuffed with mistletoe!' said Asterix, working out what the foreign servant was saying with the aid of their translator tablet. 'He must think we're on a plundering expedition, looking for gold and precious stones! Luckily, mistletoe is just what we *do* want! Come on!' And the Gauls ran down the cellar steps. There were two doors in front of them. 'Right or left, do you think?' said Asterix. 'Let's try right, right?' asked Obelix. 'Right – right!' said Asterix. ***Go to 201.***

113

As they had no translator, it was impossible to make out what the British peasant was trying to tell them – and while he was jabbering away, several large, beefy Roman soldiers emerged from the undergrowth. For a moment, they looked as surprised to see the Gauls as Asterix and Obelix were to see them. But only for a moment – then they advanced! 'Two suspicious strangers, eh, questioning one of the natives?' said the decurion in command. 'Just what for, I wonder? Well, we're taking you into custody!' 'Oh no, you're not!' said Asterix, drinking some magic potion and joining Obelix, who had already begun dealing with the Romans. In no time, they were all flat on the ground, begging for mercy, and telling the Gauls that if they wanted to find out about Boadicea, they'd better go to the fortified camp of Antirrhinum. 'Where there are more than enough men to show that couple what's what!' muttered the decurion hopefully, as Asterix, Obelix and Dogmatix started off along the road – but he found talking made his head ache so much that he thought it better to keep quiet until the headache wore off.

Remove a MAGIC POTION CARD from ASTERIX'S WAIST-SLIT. Now go to 192.

114

The Gauls had no money left for bribes – but a little thing like that was not going to stand in their way now. Drinking some magic potion, Asterix swept the soldier aside, and they went on down the cellar steps, where they saw two doors. 'Let's try the one on the right here,' said Asterix.

Remove a MAGIC POTION CARD from ASTERIX'S WAIST-SLIT. Now go to 201. (Remember: when there are no magic potion cards left in Asterix's waist-slit Operation Britain cannot go on, and you must start the game again.)

115

It was a long journey back to Londinium, but most of the Britons the Gauls met on the way were very helpful, especially when they heard how urgent it was for Asterix and Obelix to get hold of some mistletoe and take it back to Gaul for Getafix. 'Everything depends

on Londinium now!' said Asterix, as they drove towards the capital.
'You know, Obelix, I never felt so sympathetic to our friends the
pirates before . . . I've got that nasty sinking feeling myself!' Obelix
looked out of the chariot, in some alarm. 'Don't worry, it's all right,'
he said. 'We're not at sea.' 'I mean I've got a nasty sinking feeling
that when we reach the oak-wood near Londinium, we'll find its
mistletoe has gone too!' And he was quite right. 'Yes, it was a terrible
blow!' quavered the aged druid in charge of the oak-wood. 'We
heard you were coming in search of mistletoe for your druid, the
famous Getafix, and hoped you'd be here in time – but the
Governor's men arrived first, made us cut mistletoe with our golden
sickles, and took the lot. It'll be under lock and key by now!' 'Hm
. . . I wonder just *where* it's under lock and key?' Asterix said. 'The
Tower of Londinium, perhaps?' suggested the druid. 'Ooh, do let's
go to the Tower!' said Obelix. 'Remember what fun we had there
last time we came to Britain?' Leaving their chariot and horses with
the druid, the Gauls made their way to the sinister Tower of
Londinium, where ravens soared overhead – and Roman sentries
stood on guard at the gates. 'Now,' said Asterix, 'which one of us
will try getting past them first?'

**Throw the special DICE to decide who approaches the sentries
first.**

If you throw ASTERIX	go to 231
If you throw OBELIX	go to 185
If you throw DOGMATIX	go to 94

'It's military information we really want to try to pick up,' said Asterix, as the Gauls went on along the road to Durobrivae. They turned the corner of the road, and saw a large fenced enclosure ahead of them. 'That looks like a barracks to me!' said Obelix. 'So it does,' agreed Asterix. 'Just the place to find military information. Now, how shall we set about it? I don't mind volunteering to go up to the gates and try to bluff our way in!' 'Why does it always have to be you?' grumbled Obelix. 'Why not me for a change? I'm as bluff as you are any day.' And Dogmatix started barking as if to say, 'Why not me?' 'Well, if we all want to do it, the fairest way would be to draw lots,' said Asterix.

Throw the special DICE to decide who tries bluffing his way into the camp first.

If you throw ASTERIX	go to 203
If you throw OBELIX	go to 74
If you throw DOGMATIX	go to 45

117

'It's no good,' said Obelix. 'We'll never make out what McRobiotix here is saying. Nice to meet you, though, old boy!' he added, remembering British customs. 'Let me shake you by the hand!' 'Obelix!' shouted Asterix. 'Stop it! You don't know your own strength – let him go! Scot free!' 'Oh, all right,' said Obelix, freeing the badly shaken Caledonian. 'You might have saved your energies for *this* lot,' remarked Asterix a little later, as they emerged from the wood into the middle of a large body of Roman legionaries resting there. Even worse, they themselves were recognised. 'Look – two Gauls!' someone shouted. 'We're supposed to be looking out for two dangerous Gauls and a dog – and there's the dog, too!' 'So this is what McRobiotix was trying to tell us,' said Asterix grimly, as he took a magic potion and helped Obelix fight their way through the party of Romans and out the other side, so that they could walk on.

Remove a MAGIC POTION CARD from ASTERIX'S WAIST-SLIT. Now go to 255.

'I don't see why Dogmatix shouldn't get his way, after all!' said Asterix. 'Come on! Mona!' 'Who are you calling a moaner?' asked Obelix, indignantly. 'It's the name of the island,' Asterix reminded him, and they set off north-west. After a while, as they were passing through a village, Dogmatix started trying to tug Obelix towards the village shops by the seat of his trousers. 'He's telling us something. I wonder what?' said Asterix. 'I *know* what!' said Obelix. The same thought had occurred to him and Dogmatix at almost the same time. 'He's telling us we ought to stock up with provisions for the journey. Look at that pork butcher's! Doesn't the window display look nice?' And Obelix was already disappearing into the shop, smacking his lips. 'We'll have those sausages – and that leg of boar – and those pies – and –' 'And that'll be ten coins, so far,' said the pork butcher, wrapping the meat up. 'Steady on, Obelix,' said Asterix. 'Make sure we can pay before you ask for any more!'

Is OBELIX carrying a COINBAG? If so, count out the ten coins by rotating the disc, and then go to the number shown on the other side. If not, go to 145.

As they started along the road to Durobrivae, the Gauls saw several Britons having a picnic. Obelix's mouth watered when he saw that they were eating cold boar – roast, not boiled. He was very ready to accept when the picnickers invited him, Asterix and Dogmatix to join them. 'It's rather brave of you, having a picnic with so many Romans about,' said Asterix. 'Oh, it doesn't do to let the Romans spoil everything,' said one of the Britons cheerfully. 'You're Gaulish, aren't you?' 'Yes, and to tell you the truth, we're on a special mission,' said Asterix. 'Have another boar – and have this, too!' said the hospitable picnicker, offering him a password scroll. 'Some Roman soldiers dropped it passing through our village – you might find it useful.'

If OBELIX is not already carrying the PASSWORD SCROLL, put it in his WAIST-SLIT. Now go to 116.

'No, the password is not *WINE*!' said the decurion triumphantly. 'I thought you looked suspicious! You're coming back to garrison headquarters to explain yourselves, you are!' 'Oh no, we're not!' said Asterix, swallowing one of his emergency doses of magic potion. 'This is all the explanation you're getting! Come on, Obelix!' Obelix needed no further persuasion to have a bit of fun with some Romans, and the landlord of the Boar and Whistle, encouraged by the sight of the patrol being flattened, popped out of his pub with a rolling-pin in one hand and a ladle in the other to help. 'Is that all?' asked Obelix, disappointed, looking round for more Romans. 'For the moment!' said the landlord. 'But there'll be reinforcements along soon to scrape their friends off the road – you'd better not stay here! Try the Queen Boadicea – it's that way. The landlord, Beeswax, is in the British resistance. Ask him, I'm sure that he'll give you shelter.'

Remove a MAGIC POTION CARD from ASTERIX'S WAIST-SLIT. Now go to 42.

Obelix was first to see a horse-hiring stables. They went in and had two fresh horses harnessed to the borrowed chariot. The owner of the stables told them to look for a big Wall, and then they would know they were near their journey's end. As they drove out of Bravoniacum, however, they met a troop of Roman soldiers marching south. The Roman soldiers looked rather tired, which was not surprising, as they had just finished a long stint of duty, garrisoning the Wall. However, they were alert enough when confronted by the unexpected sight of Asterix and Obelix. 'Stop, you!' ordered the centurion leading them. 'That's suspiciously like an Iceni chariot! What's it doing up here – and who are *you*? You look like Gauls to me. You can't come this way unless you can give me the password.'

Is OBELIX carrying a PASSWORD SCROLL? If so, find the correct password by placing it exactly over the scroll shape on the next page – then follow the appropriate instruction. If not, you must guess which instruction to follow.

```
IA      M           B
 I  H C    P    A E
N    T  AM      E  T
ER      D     I   NG
    TOR  H        A
ND       S       W
   I   OR A     TH
 IND       IM   P
 FI       D    N
```

If you think it's CAESAR	go to 55
If you think it's CLAUDIUS	go to 106
If you think it's HADRIAN	go to 265

122

Obelix picked up the foreign servant and started shaking him. 'Stop that, Obelix!' said Asterix. 'You won't get him to speak Gaulish however hard you shake. I've an idea . . . I'm hopeless at drawing things, but I wonder if magic potion would give me artistic talent?' He drank some, and then picked up a stick of charcoal which was lying about. It worked! Asterix drew a beautiful bunch of mistletoe on the Governor's nice clean wall. The servant looked at it, and when Asterix pointed down the steps, raising his eyebrows, he nodded vigorously. The Gauls ran down the steps. 'Which of these doors shall we try?' said Asterix. 'I think the one on the left.'

Remove a MAGIC POTION CARD from ASTERIX'S

WAIST-SLIT. Now go to 79. (Remember: when there are no magic potion cards left in Asterix's waist-slit Operation Britain cannot go on, and you must start the game again.)

123

At last, driving fast, the Gauls came within sight of the magnificent Wall which stretched along the border between Caledonia and the rest of Britain. It was a fine sight, with forts set at intervals along it. Before they reached it, however, they came to a signpost put there to guide the soldiers of the garrison, and pointing to the border towns of Luguvallum, Corstopitum and Segedunum. 'Getafix told me the oak-wood is at the western end of the border,' said Asterix, 'but these roads wind so much, it's hard to see which town really *is* to the west. If you've got a map, Obelix, please look and see which of those border towns is the most westerly.'

Is OBELIX carrying a MAP? If so, consult it to see which of the three towns is the most westerly, and follow the appropriate instruction. If not, you must guess which instruction to follow.

If you think it's CORSTOPITUM   go to 213
If you think it's LUGUVALLUM   go to 250
If you think it's SEGEDUNUM   go to 67

'No money, no information!' said the villager. 'Clear off – we don't want any foreigners in this village!' 'Except Romans, I suppose, since you're so keen to stick to their rules and regulations,' said Asterix. Dogmatix added an indignant yelp, whereupon the villager kicked him. Obelix and Asterix were both furious – 'You leave this to me!' said Asterix grimly, swallowing a magic potion as Obelix bent to pick his dog up. 'And that'll teach you to kick poor dumb animals!' he told the thoroughly flattened villager a little later. 'How's Dogmatix?' he asked, as he and Obelix walked out of the village. 'Not badly hurt, except for his feelings,' said Obelix thankfully, as Dogmatix raced away ahead of them up the road that led to the fortified camp of Delphinium.

Remove a MAGIC POTION CARD from ASTERIX'S WAIST-SLIT. Now go to 160.

Obelix was chosen to approach the British peasant first. The only trouble was, he was so fascinated by the man's appearance that he forgot what it was they really wanted to know. 'Feeling blue?' he asked, sympathetically. 'No, I only look blue,' said the peasant. 'It's the woad, you know.' 'What's the matter with the road?' asked Obelix, bewildered. 'It seems all right to me, as British roads go.' 'He means woad – that blue stuff on his face!' Asterix explained. 'Wearing woad was an Ancient British custom, so Anticlimax says, though not many people keep it up nowadays. Listen, can you tell us anything about Queen Boadicea? There's a special reason we want to know.' 'Maybe I could, maybe I couldn't,' said the peasant, craftily. 'It'll cost you, though.' 'How much?' asked Asterix. 'Eight coins,' said the man.

Is OBELIX carrying a COINBAG? If so, count out the eight coins by rotating the disc, and go to the number shown on the other side. If not, go to 210.

126

'What a good thing we met that Caledonian, McRobiotix!' said Asterix as he, Obelix and Dogmatix walked out of the wood and along the road towards the town of Durobrivae. 'It's just as well he warned us that there's a great deal of Roman military activity in these parts at present – and it's useful to know he thinks we might pick up some useful bits of information if we went towards Durobrivae.' *Go to 116.*

'Oh, really, this is just too frustrating!' said Obelix, unable to make out what the waiter was saying. 'Boiled boar – over-boiled boar, at that! And now rotten service! I mean, what good is a waiter who can't speak anything but Ancient Spanish? If I shake him a bit, perhaps he'll start talking Gaulish!' 'Obelix, that is *not* the way to teach people foreign languages – Obelix, *no!*' shouted Asterix. But it was too late. Obelix was shaking the unfortunate waiter as if he were a Roman. 'Here, what's all this?' said the manager angrily, coming up. 'Put my waiter down! Help!' he shouted, and a party of Roman soldiers, dining at another table, got up and came over. 'Obelix, did you *have* to draw attention to us like this?' groaned Asterix, drinking some magic potion so that he could get Obelix safely out of the restaurant. 'Back to the chariot, and let's go on up the Fosse Way to Lindum – I think that's in the direction of Caledonia.'

Remove a *MAGIC POTION CARD* from *ASTERIX'S WAIST-SLIT*. Now go to 180.

128

As the Gauls had no translator to give them any clue as to what the innkeeper and his shifty companion were saying, they went on with their meal, but Asterix kept a close eye on the couple. He was not altogether surprised when the innkeeper moved unobtrusively to lock the front door of his inn, while his companion disappeared into the kitchen. 'Be prepared!' he whispered to Obelix – and when, next moment, a dozen hefty Roman legionaries burst into the room, they *were* prepared. Asterix had a gourd of magic potion at the ready, and swallowed its contents in one gulp before he and Obelix turned to deal with the Romans. 'That was nicer than the landlord's boiled boar!' said Obelix, pleased, as they raced away with Dogmatix, who had done his bit in the fight too, running along behind them.

Remove a MAGIC POTION CARD from ASTERIX'S WAIST-SLIT. Now go to 18.

129

'My plan,' said Obelix, 'is to sign on a Roman galley as sailors, overpower the crew once we're at sea and make them take us to Britain! Subtle, eh?' But the first Roman sea captain they approached recognised them as wanted men. 'Seize those Gauls!' he shouted. 'Come on, quick!' said Asterix. 'We don't want to be delayed now – let's find a little jolly-boat!' He ran off, followed by the others, but in all the hurry and bustle of the port, they couldn't find their way down to the beach, and asked a passer-by. He turned out to be a foreigner. 'I can't make out what he's saying – have you got a translator tablet, Obelix?' asked Asterix.

Is OBELIX carrying a TRANSLATOR? If so, use it to discover what the foreigner was saying. If not, go to 8.

Asterix gave the correct password – *CLAUDIUS*. 'There, you see!' he told the decurion. 'We're Gauls loyal to Rome – in fact, we've come over specially, with a message for the Governor in Londinium about those two dangerous Gauls you mentioned, so you'd better let us by, fast. We're in a hurry, and our message can't wait!' His moustache bristled so fiercely that the decurion apologised for not believing him at first. 'You'd better take this bag of coins, to help you get to Londinium,' he said. 'Thanks!' said Asterix, and the Gauls hurried off with the money. 'Well, now we can offer to pay for a good night's rest at a friendly British house before we go on to Cantium! Look – isn't that a sign saying BED AND BREAKFAST?'

If OBELIX is not already carrying it, put the COINBAG in his WAIST-SLIT. Now go to 109.

As they had no map, the Gauls were still none the wiser about the movement of Roman troops in Britain – and the British villager suddenly became rather less friendly. 'How do I know you're really what you say you are?' he inquired. 'You could be spies! Here – come and seize these men!' he suddenly shouted, and hordes of Britons came pouring out of the houses in the village. 'Oh no – they must all be collaborators!' said Asterix in dismay, quickly knocking back a gourd of magic potion. 'Come on, Obelix, let's clear out of here, quick, and then start on our way back to Anticlimax's village.' He went on making plans, as he and Obelix fought off the British collaborators. 'We might have another shot at getting into one of those Roman camps on the way – I think Delphinium would be the nearest.'

Remove a MAGIC POTION CARD from ASTERIX'S WAIST-SLIT. Now go to 160.

Ekonomikrisis could not come right in to shore at the port of Anderida, but he had the Gauls rowed to land in a little dinghy. They watched him sail away. 'Now then,' said Asterix, 'we need somewhere to stay the night. We must find out the way to Anticlimax's village, too – that's our first port of call. Well, our second, after Anderida.' Walking inland, they found an ancient Briton watering his garden, and decided to ask him the way – but would he be friendly or not, and which of them should approach him first?

Throw the special DICE to decide who approaches the Briton.

If you throw ASTERIX	go to 147
If you throw OBELIX	go to 188
If you throw DOGMATIX	go to 230

As the Gauls couldn't understand a word Captain Poisonus Oystus said, they hesitated, wondering which way to go. That gave the centurion time for some second thoughts about these simple Gaulish fishermen. 'Here, haven't I seen you two before somewhere?' he asked. 'When I was stationed at Aquarium, having one Hades of a time with that wretched little Gaulish village Caesar is so keen to conquer? You're coming aboard for further questioning, you are!' But Asterix had other ideas! Telling Obelix to start rowing, fast, he gulped down a dose of magic potion, snatched up a second pair of oars, and began rowing too. The superhuman strength of the Gaulish oarsmen meant they could outdistance even a Roman galley as they rowed away north and then turned east.

Remove a MAGIC POTION CARD from ASTERIX'S WAIST-SLIT. Now go to 92.

134

'Oh dear!' exclaimed Asterix. 'They *did* hear of our mission through the British underground – but the Romans knew too. We guessed that all along, from the way we've been challenged during our travels. And only a couple of days ago, Governor Encyclopaedicus Britannicus sent men to Mona, to force the Welsh druids, at spear-point, to cut their mistletoe crop and hand it over! They say he made the druids of the Caledonian wood cut all their mistletoe and confiscated that too!' 'Now what?' said Obelix. 'Now we'll just have to go back to Londinium,' said Asterix. 'At least we can give you this,' said the leader of the Welsh druids, giving the Gauls a password scroll. 'It may help you to track the mistletoe down.'

If OBELIX is not already carrying the PASSWORD SCROLL, put it in his WAIST-SLIT. Then go to 115.

Dogmatix started barking excitedly – he had been the first to see a
stables that hired out horses. Asterix and Obelix could understand
him all right when he barked like that, but it turned out they couldn't
understand a word the owner of the stable said. He put a fresh pair of
horses between the shafts of the chariot for them, but when they
asked him the way to the border of Caledonia, they couldn't make
head or tail of his answer. 'Have we got a translator tablet, Obelix?
That might help,' said Asterix.

*Is OBELIX carrying a TRANSLATOR? If so, use it to find out
what the man is saying in the picture below, and follow the
instruction in the speech bubble. If not, go to 43.*

136

The Gauls had no money, and Obelix was just about to flatten the
Roman legionary and march on into the cellar, when the man
suddenly dodged and ran up the steps, shouting for help. But other
voices could be heard shouting outside too, amidst the sound of
chariot wheels and the tramp of marching feet. *Go to 218.*

Dogmatix chased hopefully up to a steak-house. 'All right, Dogmatix!' said Asterix. 'I expect we can get a reasonable meal here – and a couple of nice bones for you!' They ate a large dinner, but there was a nasty surprise at the end of it: the bill. 'You know what?' said Asterix, looking at it in dismay. 'We're so used to *catching* our dinner, I quite forgot about having to *pay*. They want six coins. Have we got a coinbag?'

Is OBELIX carrying a COINBAG? If so, count out the six coins by rotating the disc, and go to the number shown on the other side. If not, go to 189.

138

There was no way of understanding what the sentries were saying. 'And things are getting pretty urgent,' said Asterix. 'Everything indicates that the village is to be attacked quite soon – we need more information! This calls for magic potion!' He drank some, and both Gauls marched boldly into the camp, followed just as boldly by Dogmatix. Seizing the nearest Roman soldiers, they shook them gently until they promised to tell all they knew. 'Well, well!' said Asterix, as he and Obelix left the camp of Delphinium again. 'So a big attack on the village is planned for tomorrow. Our information-gathering expedition has been successful after all!'

Remove a MAGIC POTION CARD from ASTERIX'S WAIST-SLIT. Now go to 211.

'Twenty coins, just to row over our own bit of sea between Gaul and Britain?' said Obelix, indignantly. 'These Normans are crazy!' He was about to board their ship and knock Timandahaf down. All the Normans clustered at the longship's rail, looking very threatening. Just then, however, a wind got up, and they had to see to the great sail of their ship. 'Come on, Obelix, row!' urged Asterix. Obelix bent to the oars, and while the Normans were busy with their sail, the Gauls shot off over the Mare Britannicum. *Go to 92.*

As the Gauls went down the road to Chrysanthemum, which Dogmatix seemed to think would be the best camp to visit, they tried to think of a good excuse for wanting to go in. 'We ought to have Roman disguises, or something,' said Asterix. 'I suppose we'll just have to pretend to be tourists.' But before they reached the camp, they found a barrier across the road, and a man standing beside it told them they would have to pay a toll to go up to the camp gates. 'How much?' asked Asterix. 'Nine coins for the three of you – three each,' said the toll-collector.

Is OBELIX carrying a COINBAG? If so, count out nine coins by rotating the disc, and then go to the number shown on the opposite side. If not, go to 184.

141

They set off along the road leading to Londinium, but the farther they went that way, the more Roman soldiers they saw on the same road. 'I suppose they're on their way back to barracks now that dusk is falling,' said Asterix. 'I doubt if this is the best way to Anticlimax's village after all. I think we'd do better to turn back and try the Durovernum road instead.' So they did – but before they had reached the signpost where the three roads met, Obelix suddenly bent down and picked something up. 'Look, this was lying in the road! A Roman must have dropped it as he marched along,' he said. 'Why, it's a scroll listing the passwords the Roman army in Britain is using this week!' said Asterix. 'What a bit of luck! Let's take it with us.'

If OBELIX is not already carrying the PASSWORD SCROLL, put it in his WAIST-SLIT. Now go to 72.

142

Ekonomikrisis put the Gauls ashore at Portus Adurni before sailing away to trade his cargo for tin. 'You know, we seem to have sailed quite a long way westward along the south coast of Britain,' said Asterix, squinting up at the sky. 'I'm sure we ought to turn back east for Cantium and my cousin's village – we want to go there for advice before we start looking for that magic mistletoe.' So they turned east, and soon came to a place where three roads met. 'I think this is probably the right road,' said Asterix, glancing at the sky again. 'No, this one!' said Obelix. 'Don't ask me why – I just *feel* I'm right!' And Dogmatix kept making little dashes down the third road and coming back to the Gauls, as if telling them to follow him. Which road should they choose?

Throw the special DICE to decide whose choice of road the Gauls will take.

If you throw ASTERIX   go to 279
If you throw OBELIX   go to 102
If you throw DOGMATIX   go to 237

143

It was decided that Asterix would approach the peasant first and see what information he could get about Boadicea. 'Oh yes,' said the peasant, trying to be helpful. 'Reckon I've heard of her, right enough! Sacked some Roman town, didn't she? Near the east coast.' 'What was its name?' asked Asterix. 'That could be a useful bit of information too,' he told Obelix and Dogmatix. 'Ah now – its name! Well, that I can't rightly remember,' said the peasant. 'Was it

Glevum? Or maybe Camulodunum? Or it could have been Verulamium. It was near the east coast, though, that's for sure. If you had a map, maybe you could tell which of those she sacked.'

Is OBELIX carrying a MAP? If so, use it to find out which of the towns mentioned is nearest to the east coast of Britain, and follow the appropriate instruction. If not, you'll have to guess which instruction to follow.

If you think it's CAMULODUNUM	go to 222
If you think it's GLEVUM	go to 178
If you think it's VERULAMIUM	go to 161

144

As they drove on towards Glevum, they passed through a forest, and met an old charcoal-burner who told them they were on the wrong road. 'It's Lindum you want,' he said, and he told them a short cut back to the Fosse Way. Unfortunately, they found the way blocked by some large fallen trees, so many of them that it would take even Obelix a long time to clear them away on his own. 'We mustn't waste too much time,' said Asterix, and he decided to take some magic potion and help his friend, so that they could drive on to Lindum without more delay.

Remove a MAGIC POTION CARD from ASTERIX'S WAIST-SLIT. Now go to 180.

'Pay?' said Obelix. He searched his pockets, but there was no coinbag there. 'Oh dear. I forgot about paying.' He looked so sad as the pork butcher began unwrapping all the lovely meat and pies and sausages again that Asterix impulsively offered the butcher some magic potion. 'Would you take this instead of money?' he asked. 'It's magic, you know – brewed by the famous Gaulish druid Getafix.' 'Brewed by Getafix? Then you must be Asterix and Obelix!' exclaimed the butcher. 'I shall keep this magic potion as a family heirloom. Going to Mona, you say? Well, carry on along this road, until you come to a place where two large main roads meet.'

Remove a MAGIC POTION CARD from ASTERIX'S WAIST-SLIT. Now go to 107.

'He recommends Portus Adurni as a good place for your ship to put in,' Obelix told Ekonomikrisis. 'He says it has a good big harbour.' 'Thank you,' Asterix said politely to the seaman, and the Phoenician vessel turned away, much to the relief of Captain Nautilus. **Go to 142.**

'Excuse me,' said Asterix politely, going up to the ancient Briton, 'but could you tell me the way to Anticlimax's village?' 'What? Who? Where?' asked the ancient Briton, who was a little hard of hearing. 'Yes, that's what we were asking you,' said Asterix. 'Where is it?' 'Where's what, what?' When they had finally got themselves straightened out, the ancient Briton asked the name of the village where Anticlimax lived. 'Do you know, I never found out!' Asterix realised. 'You don't know its name? Then what's the nearest town?' asked the Briton. He was a countryman himself, he added, and didn't know many towns, but he mentioned three he *had* heard of, pointing in their general direction. They were Verulamium, Portus Lemanis and Durovernum. 'Have you got a map, Obelix?' asked Asterix.

Is OBELIX carrying a MAP? If so, look to see which of the three towns is nearest to Anticlimax's village, and follow the appropriate instruction. If not, you must guess which instruction to follow.

If you think it's DUROVERNUM	go to 32
If you think it's PORTUS LEMANIS	go to 100
If you think it's VERULAMIUM	go to 166

148

'I'm still not sure we translated what that Briton was saying correctly,' said Obelix, as they began walking up some hills, the way he had told them to go. 'I mean, whoever heard of hills called Downs? Anyone can see that hills go up!' 'Well, this is definitely the way he said,' said Asterix, 'and he told us where we could find a hut in these hills to spend the night, too. I say – look at this! We really are in luck!' he added, bending to pick up something lying by the roadside. 'A bag of coins! I hope it belonged to Romans, not Britons – but we'll take it with us, all in a good cause!'

If OBELIX is not already carrying the COINBAG, put it into his WAIST-SLIT. Now go to 149.

149

The Gauls had a good night's rest in the hut they found on the hills called the Downs. As there were goats on the hillside, they had goat's milk for breakfast. 'That's better!' said Asterix, as they set off again. 'And now let's go straight to Anticlimax's village. I can steer our way by the sun from here!' They were not far from the village, by Asterix's reckoning, when they rounded a corner and found a fortified Roman camp right in their path. 'Goodness me – I'm sure there wasn't a Roman camp here before!' said the surprised Asterix. But they were already being challenged by the guards at the gate. Apparently no one was allowed past the camp unless they could give the password.

*Is **OBELIX** carrying a **PASSWORD SCROLL**? If so, use it to find out the correct password by placing it exactly over the scroll shape below. Then follow the appropriate instruction. If not, you must guess which instruction to follow.*

```
        B           A
    A     R     R     E     L B
  Z     U     L     J
  Y   P   E   8   9   Z
      M       O   Y P
    X T     D U     L Z
    B     R A I     O     9
    6     7     R     E       Z
    3   R O       P L     7
```

If you think it's BARLEY	go to 181
If you think it's OATS	go to 215
If you think it's WHEAT	go to 196

'Is the password *BEER*?' said Asterix. 'No,' said the sentries. 'Thought you wouldn't know it! Like we said, you can't come in, so shove off!' 'Tut, tut – such language!' said Asterix, severely, drinking some magic potion. 'Come along, Obelix, let's shove *them* off and see what's inside this Tower!' The answer to that was a lot of Roman soldiers. 'Mucus, don't you think those two men somehow looked familiar?' said one of the sentries, faintly, trying to sit up. 'Yes, Porus,' groaned his companion, feeling the bump on his head. 'They visited the Tower once before! Just our luck to be on sentry duty again!' The Gauls were even more recognisable when they emerged again, with Obelix carrying a vast pile of helmets – but no mistletoe. 'Now then!' said Asterix to the battered sentries. 'We know Governor Encyclopaedicus has all the magic mistletoe in Britain stored somewhere in Londinium – but it's not here, so where is it?' 'In his palace, and please, *please* go away now!' begged the sentries. 'Anything to oblige!' said Asterix. 'Come on, Obelix, we're off to the Governor's palace.'

Remove a *MAGIC POTION CARD* from *ASTERIX'S WAIST-SLIT*. Now go to 2. (Remember: when there are no magic potion cards left in Asterix's waist-slit Operation Britain cannot go on, and you must start the game again.)

'I'm sorry,' said Obelix. 'We just haven't got the money to pay for your fish.' And he did look sorry – Asterix could hardly bear to see his friend's face. He knew he ought to be keeping his magic potion for emergencies, but if ever there *was* an emergency, Obelix suffering the pangs of hunger was it! 'Here!' he said, offering the fishmonger a gourd of potion. 'This is the famous magic potion our druid brews in Gaul . . . oh, it's a long story, but let us have some fish, and this will pay for it.' When Fishcax had heard all about Operation Britain, he suggested that they could go to the camp of Chrysanthemum, where a lot of Roman soldiers had been gathering recently. 'I won't say I'm not glad of your potion,' he added, 'because life's dangerous for an undercover agent these days. But go very carefully, and do take just as many fish as you want in return for it!'

Remove a MAGIC POTION CARD from ASTERIX'S WAIST-SLIT. Now go to 171.

'*PARSLEY*!' said Asterix, giving the correct password, and walking into the cellar – where they met Governor Encyclopaedicus

Britannicus himself, gloating over the piles of mistletoe. 'Ho, ho, ho!' he was chuckling. 'The Gauls will never be able to make their magic potion now – and won't Caesar be pleased with me for foiling them! Maybe I'll get recalled to Rome, and never have to eat boiled boar again! The Gauls . . . help! The Gauls!' he exclaimed, seeing them. 'Asterix and Obelix, from their description! Help! Help! Help!' 'Sorry, Encyclopaedicus, old chap,' said Asterix, 'but I'd say Caesar's more likely to recall you to Rome for a date in the Circus, with the lions!' 'Help! Help! Dangerous Gauls!' the Governor kept shouting, so Obelix gagged him, just as if he were Cacofonix. *Go to 235.*

153

The Gauls soon reached the town of Deva. 'Not so very far to Mona now,' said Asterix. 'Then we can ask the druids there to give us mistletoe and take it home to Getafix!' He spoke too soon. As they drove their chariot into Deva, they were met by a deputation of Welsh druids. 'They must have heard of our mission through the British underground, and they've come to meet us!' exclaimed Asterix. 'How nice of them!' 'Perhaps they've even brought the mistletoe?' suggested Obelix. 'Perhaps – but I don't see any, do you? And their faces look very solemn,' said Asterix. 'I wish to

Toutatis I knew what their leader is saying! Have you got a translator tablet, Obelix?'

Is OBELIX carrying a TRANSLATOR? If so, use it to find out what the druid is saying in the picture below, and follow the instruction in the speech bubble. If not, go to 6.

154

'So he says Queen Boadicea has been doing heroic deeds, though he's not sure what,' said Asterix, consulting the translator. The man said something else. 'And he thinks we might find out more if we go to the nearest Roman camp, Antirrhinum. Well, that's useful to know – let's try Antirrhinum. Well done, Dogmatix!' he added. The little dog thumped his tail again with pleasure at Asterix's praise. *Go to 192.*

They decided to try going towards Deva, but they had not gone far when a wheel came off their borrowed chariot. 'What a nuisance!' said Asterix. 'If we're going all the way to Caledonia, we can't afford to hang about here. I'll take some magic potion, and then I can carry the chariot to the nearest wheelwright's while you carry the horses, Obelix.' They soon found a wheelwright, but he told them they were going the wrong way for Caledonia, and once he had mended the chariot, he showed them the road north to Lindum.

Remove a MAGIC POTION CARD from ASTERIX'S WAIST-SLIT. Now go to 180.

156

'Viroconium is the place we should be making for, on our way to the island of Mona,' said Asterix, folding up the map again. 'Right, we go on along Watling Street.' 'It's fun driving a chariot and pair down a Roman road,' agreed Obelix. 'Yes, but we mustn't forget this is Operation Britain, not a pleasure trip,' Asterix reminded him. 'You've already had your fun, thumping Romans at the battle for Anticlimax's village! Still, I'll admit I'm beginning to feel quite hopeful about the success of our mistletoe mission. We'll soon reach Viroconium – and then we're bound for Mona.' ***Go to 38.***

The foreigner was telling them the way down to the beach . . . not only that, but he seemed anxious to press a bag of coins into their hands, and wouldn't take no for an answer. 'He seems to think we're business contacts of his,' said Asterix. 'Oh, well – we'll get him to write his name down, and then we can return the money later!' 'I hope *you* can read that, Asterix,' said Obelix doubtfully, looking at the hieroglyphic signature. But by now Dogmatix was racing ahead of them down to the beach, and he soon sniffed out a friendly Gaul with boats for hire.

If OBELIX is not already carrying the COINBAG, put it into his WAIST-SLIT, and go to 51.

Asterix reached the mushrooms first and began picking them. The others helped him, and everyone had a nibble or so of raw mushroom, though they tied most of them up in a handkerchief to be taken back to the village. Still looking for mushrooms, they came out at the far side of the wood, and saw a signpost. 'Why don't we try going a little closer to Londinium? That's where Roman head-quarters is,' said Asterix, 'and we might find out more if we went that way.' The signpost pointed to Durobrivae, Noviomagus and Calleva. 'Now I wonder which of those is closest to Londinium? Have you got a map, Obelix?'

Is OBELIX carrying a MAP? If so, consult it to find out which town is closest to Londinium and follow the appropriate instruction. If not, you must guess which instruction to follow.

If you think it's CALLEVA	go to 281
If you think it's DUROBRIVAE	go to 119
If you think it's NOVIOMAGUS	go to 163

'*BEER* is wrong,' said the guard. 'Especially warm beer,' agreed Obelix. 'Tourists you may be,' the guard went on, 'but that doesn't give you any right to walk round Roman army camps! Whoever heard of such a thing?' 'Oh, we've often done it before,' said Obelix. 'You have to get inside Roman army camps if you want to thump the legionaries there, see?' 'If you want to do *what*?' said the astonished guard. 'Shut up, Obelix!' hissed Asterix. 'Come on, quick – it's no good trying to get in here, not if you're going to say that sort of thing!' 'I was only telling the truth – don't you approve of that?' said Obelix, following Asterix to a little wood some way off. *Go to 3.*

As they approached the fortified camp of Delphinium, the Gauls left the main road. 'We don't want to be seen around here by too many Romans,' said Asterix. Dogmatix suddenly started barking, and raced off. 'He's seen a nice tree!' said Obelix. 'You know how Dogmatix loves a nice tree!' The tree was a big lime, with its lower branches drooping right down to the ground. 'We could hide quite well in there!' said Asterix. 'It's like a tent of leaves. Why don't we sit under the tree and see if there's any noticeable sort of activity inside the camp? Well done, Dogmatix!' They discovered that from under the tree, they could even hear what the two sentries on guard at the camp gates were saying to each other . . . the only trouble was, the sentries were speaking a language the Gauls didn't understand. 'I think it's Thracian,' said Asterix. 'The Roman army recruits a lot of Thracians. We need a translator to understand them!'

Is OBELIX carrying a TRANSLATOR? If so, use it to find out what the sentry is saying in the picture below, and follow the instruction given in his speech bubble. If not, go to 138.

'Well, if you haven't got a map, I reckon I can't be much more help,' said the peasant. 'Wait a moment . . . I'm pretty sure it wasn't Glevum, but which of the other two towns it *was*, I'm sure I can't say!' 'Maybe our best plan would be to go back to the Roman fortified camps,' suggested Asterix. 'Antirrhinum's that way,' the peasant told him, pointing to a winding country road. ***Go to 192.***

It turned out that the man was warning them they couldn't get much farther along the road ahead, because of a flood. 'I wonder what we ought to do?' said Asterix. He turned to the man, and using the translator, asked if he had seen any of the anti-Roman type of Britons in the area. The merchant thought for a bit, and then told them where to find the camp of Queen Boadicea and her tribe, the Iceni. He was so pleased to find somebody speaking his own language to him that he insisted on giving the Gauls a useful password scroll he had brought on his travels in Britain.

If OBELIX is not already carrying the PASSWORD SCROLL, put it in his WAIST-SLIT. Then go to 200.

The Gauls had gone a little way down the road to Noviomagus when they turned a corner and saw Roman troops marching towards them. 'Romans!' said Obelix gleefully. 'Lots of lovely Romans! Let's get them!' 'No, let's not!' said Asterix. 'We're trying to gather information on the quiet, remember? There's nothing very quiet about the way you thump Romans! I don't know that this road was such a good idea after all – let's try the road to Durobrivae instead!' Turning back, however, they found another large body of Roman troops marching along the road the other way. 'See? We've *got* to thump some Romans now!' said Obelix happily. Asterix had to admit he was right – he drank some magic potion, and they fought their way through the advancing Romans and back on to the road to Durobrivae.

Remove a MAGIC POTION CARD from ASTERIX'S WAIST-SLIT. Now go to 116.

'*THYME*'s wrong – thyme you were on your way,' said the Roman guard, laughing. 'This is no joke!' said Asterix grimly, and he and Obelix were about to force their way past the guards and into the cellar full of mistletoe, when they heard a sudden noise – it sounded like chariots driving up outside, together with the clash of armour, and raised voices. *Go to 218.*

'Are you sure you said *WHEAT*?' inquired the decurion. The Gauls looked very suspicious to him – but they had given the correct password after all. 'Very well, you can pass!' he told them grudgingly. Down by the sea, just as Asterix expected, they found rowing boats, and hired one. 'It's a jolly little jolly-boat,' said Obelix, getting in. 'Good thing we're travelling light!' he added, as his end of the boat dipped right down into the water. *Go to 51.*

Since they hadn't got a map, they were not much wiser than before, but they thanked the ancient Briton for his help, and decided to try going north, towards Verulamium. As dusk began to fall, they came to some hills. They also came to a party of Roman soldiers marching south to Anderida. 'Halt!' yelled the burly centurion in charge, seeing two civilians. 'I'm Centurion Bumptius, commanding the garrison of Anderida – and who might *you* be?' 'Er – we're tourists,' said Asterix. 'Oh yes?' said Bumptius. 'That's right!' said Asterix. 'We're innocent tourists. For instance, we were just admiring these hills. Can you tell us what they're called?' 'Yes,' said the centurion, 'they're the Downs.' 'Come off it!' said Obelix disbelievingly. 'Anyone can see they're ups, not downs! You're having us on. But maybe you can tell us if we're going the right way for the little rebel village still holding out against the Roman invaders – ouch!' he finished as Asterix dug him sharply in the ribs. The Romans fell about laughing at the notion that due north was the way to the village . . . once they had finished laughing, however, what Obelix had said sank in. 'And just what would you want with those rebels, if you're innocent tourists?' inquired Bumptious. 'Men – GET

THEM!' Just in time, Asterix swallowed some magic potion, and he and Obelix waded into Bumptius and his men. 'I don't think Verulamium's right after all,' said Asterix, a little later. 'We ought not to have stunned *all* the Romans – they could have told us the way. Let's go on into the hills. I can see a shepherd's hut where we might spend the night.'

Remove a *MAGIC POTION CARD* from *ASTERIX'S WAIST-SLIT*. Now go to 149.

167

The Gauls decided to try the road to Danum. Before they had got very far, they found a number of Britons standing about in a green field with a bat, a ball, and three sticks stuck in the ground. 'Let's just ask this druid in the white robe if we're going the right way,' said Asterix. 'Sorry, I'm umpiring. Can't tell you till the game's over,' said the druid. 'Oh, it's a game, is it?' said Asterix. Most of the Britons were just standing there, doing nothing much, but every now and then one of them ran up and threw the ball at the man with the bat, who tried not to let it hit the sticks. 'How long will it go on?' Obelix asked. 'Three days,' said the druid. 'It's a county match.'

'Three *days*, for a game?' said the astonished Asterix. 'We can talk at the end of the innings, though,' the druid added. 'And how long does an innings last?' asked Asterix. 'Until ten out of eleven men are out,' said the druid. 'Right!' said Asterix, swallowing some magic potion. 'Give me that ball!' He threw it at the sticks ten times, hit them ten times, and then the umpire was free to tell him he was going the wrong way. Resisting all the Britons' efforts to sign him on to stand about in a green field doing nothing much all summer, Asterix turned the chariot. 'Off we go to Deva!' he said.

Remove a *MAGIC POTION CARD* from *ASTERIX'S WAIST-SLIT*. Now go to 153.

168

The Gauls left the Chariot and Horses, and set off towards Rutupiae. Before very long, however, Asterix looked up at the sun, worked out the points of the compass, and said, 'Bother – I'm afraid this can't be the right way. We want to go in more of a north-easterly direction for Londinium.' They went into another inn, just to check that Asterix was right, and had a nasty surprise when a large man armed with a sword jumped at them. He was a Roman centurion on leave who had heard the two Gauls were wanted, and recognised them. This fight was one Asterix had to take on, since Obelix, though immensely strong, was not much of a fencer. 'I'll have to drink a magic potion,' said Asterix, and once he had, the result was a foregone conclusion. They set off along the road again.

Remove a MAGIC POTION CARD from ASTERIX'S WAIST-SLIT. Now go to 18.

169

'No, *PARSLEY*'s wrong!' said the innkeeper, with a triumphant note in his voice, and Asterix soon saw why when the man suddenly whistled. It must have been a prearranged signal, because several large, fully armed Romans suddenly came striding out of the back quarters of the inn and stationed themselves between the Gauls and the doorway. 'Here you are – two suspicious characters who don't know the proper password!' said the landlord. 'And if I'm not much mistaken,' said the leader of the Romans, who had seen the latest "Wanted" list, 'two *very* suspicious Gaulish characters sought by the authorities in Londinium.' With so many Romans between them and the door, the Gauls were in a trap – Asterix had to drink some magic potion before he, Obelix and Dogmatix could break out of it and get safely away.

Remove a **MAGIC POTION CARD** *from* **ASTERIX'S WAIST-SLIT**. *Now go to 228.*

170

'*BEER* it is,' said the Iceni, looking and sounding much friendlier than before. 'You must be allies after all! You say you're looking for mistletoe so that your druid can go on making magic potion? Come along up to the fort and meet Queen Boadicea. She's sure to be able to give you good advice.' **Go to 200.**

171

Outside the fortified camp of Chrysanthemum, the Gauls met a squad of reinforcements marching in – and as luck would have it, they were led by a Roman whose face Asterix and Obelix knew. It was Centurion Gracchus Armisurplus, who had once been stationed in Gaul . . . and he knew *their* faces too. 'Indomitable Armorican Gauls, by Jupiter!' he exclaimed. 'What are you doing

here?' 'We're on a sight-seeing tour of the British Isles, that's all!'
Asterix protested. 'Oh yes?' said Armisurplus. 'I don't believe a
word of it! I bet you don't even know whether Glevum, Ratae or
Habitancum is in Caledonia – one of them is, the others aren't. Well,
do you know?'

**Is OBELIX carrying a MAP? If so, consult it to see which of the
towns is in Caledonia and follow the appropriate instruction. If
not, you must guess which instruction to follow.**

If you think it's GLEVUM	go to 39
If you think it's HABITANCUM	go to 259
If you think it's RATAE	go to 243

172

What with all that rowing, and the sea air, Asterix, Obelix and
Dogmatix were feeling hungry by the time they landed in Dubris. 'I
could eat anything,' said Obelix. 'Even boiled boar with mint
sauce!' Evening was coming on, too, and they realised they must
find a place to stay the night. They walked through the town,
hoping to find an inn. 'Let's try that one – the Queen Boadicea,'
suggested Asterix. 'It looks a nice quiet sort of place.' 'Or there's one
called the Boar and Whistle down this road,' said Obelix. 'I like the

sound of that!' Dogmatix stopped to bark hopefully up at the sign of an inn called the Dog and Dux. How were they to make up their minds which inn to try?

Throw the special DICE to decide whose choice of inn the Gauls will visit.

If you throw ASTERIX   go to 103
If you throw OBELIX   go to 174
If you throw DOGMATIX   go to 241

173

'Well, that bit of bluff worked all right!' said Asterix. 'We took the guards by surprise, and they never had time to ask for any proof that we actually *are* plumbers! Here are the steps down to the palace cellars! Who's going down first?'

Throw the special DICE to decide who goes down the cellar steps first.

If you throw ASTERIX   go to 268
If you throw OBELIX   go to 177
If you throw DOGMATIX   go to 267

174

'Come on, let's try the Boar and Whistle. It sounds hopeful!' said Obelix, heading for the inn. But just as they reached it, the landlord pulled the shutters down. 'Sorry, old chap, we're closing for the night!' he told Obelix. 'Roman curfew, don't you know, what! The

Romans are getting very strict about closing time.' 'Oh, what a bore!' said Obelix crossly, looking up at the inn sign. The landlord was right, however; a Roman patrol came marching down the street at that very moment. 'Halt, you!' shouted the decurion commanding the patrol. 'You two look like Gauls to me. And what might you be doing out and about in the streets of Dubris at this time of night? Do you know the password, eh?'

If OBELIX is carrying a PASSWORD SCROLL, use it to find out the correct password by placing it exactly over the scroll shape below, and then follow the appropriate instruction. If not, you must guess which instruction to follow.

```
    U     N     S      EU
       M     L     E       T
    R    EV     O    U
       S     E     M       A
    NQ     U        E     E
       T        TO     U
    T      E     A      ST
    DE  P        EU      P
       L     E          D
```

If you think it's BEER	go to 207
If you think it's MEAD	go to 245
If you think it's WINE	go to 120

Without a translator tablet, the Gauls couldn't make out what on earth the chariot conductor was saying. But he kept pointing as the chariot went along. 'See that handsome house there?' said Asterix. 'I'm sure he's pointing at that – and isn't it the Governor's palace? Since the mistletoe wasn't in the Tower, it's more than likely that Encyclopaedicus Britannicus wants it where he can keep an eye on it. Come on – let's go to the palace!' They got off the chariot – and walked straight into a Roman patrol. 'Seize those men!' cried the decurion in command, recognising their Gaulish helmets. But Asterix didn't want to be held up at this point. Drinking a magic potion, he helped Obelix clear the road of legionaries, and they raced on towards the Governor's palace.

Remove a MAGIC POTION CARD from ASTERIX'S WAIST-SLIT. Now go to 2. (Remember: when there are no magic potion cards left in Asterix's waist-slit Operation Britain cannot go on, and you must start the game again.)

'You were bluffing!' Captain Nautilus accused Asterix. 'The password isn't *MISTLETOE*, and I don't think this vessel belongs to a friendly power at all – it's probably a spy ship.' Ekonomikrisis thought it was time he intervened. 'No, really, sir,' he said, 'my friend here was telling the truth. Look, this proves it: a nice bale of purple cloth from Tyre . . . it's very tiresome, but I'll let you keep it if you like,' he added, reluctantly. Pleased with this handsome present, Captain Nautilus let the ship pass after all. 'We're not too far from Anderida,' said the Phoenician. 'I might as well drop you off there.' ***Go to 132.***

Obelix led the way down the cellar steps, only to find himself confronted by a Palace servant telling them something which amused him – the trouble was, the servant spoke a language he couldn't understand. 'I can't make it out either,' said Asterix.

Is OBELIX carrying a TRANSLATOR? If so, use it to find out what the servant is saying in the picture below, and go to the number given in the speech bubble. If not, go to 122 instead.

SUT LIM IGI HOS TUL BAS

The Gauls had no map, and though the peasant racked his brains, he simply couldn't remember the name of the town Boadicea had sacked. 'I tell you who could very likely give you news of it, though,' he said. 'A large body of legionaries went marching down that road a little while ago – yes, that one over there!' And he pointed to it. 'It goes to the camp of Antirrhinum.' 'Hm, yes,' said Asterix. 'If we follow the legionaries we might well find out more about the military situation in Britain.' *Go to 192.*

They couldn't understand a word the centurion was saying – but it did not sound friendly. And Dogmatix was running on and on across the barracks square. 'He's probably on the scent of a secret weapon!' said Obelix, proudly. 'Well, the Romans are hardly likely to let *us* get a look at any secret weapons,' Asterix pointed out. 'Whistle him to heel!' Reluctantly, Obelix did – and Dogmatix rejoined them just as armed legionaries, summoned by the centurion, came up from all sides. 'Oh dear – I suppose I'll have to drink some magic potion to help us get out of this!' sighed Asterix. 'Well,' he added, a little later, as they left a great heap of bruised and battered legionaries piled in the middle of the barracks square behind them, 'I suppose the only thing we can do now is walk round the outside.'

Remove a *MAGIC POTION CARD* from *ASTERIX'S WAIST-SLIT*. Now go to 11.

They arrived at the town of Lindum by nightfall. 'Queen Boadicea's chariot is a great help on our mistletoe mission,' said Asterix. 'If we rest this pair of horses overnight, and make sure they have a good feed, they'll be able to carry us over the next stage of our journey tomorrow.' 'Don't forget about a good feed for us too,' said Obelix. Dogmatix barked, hopefully. They found an inn where they could get a meal and a good night's rest, and set off again next morning. The innkeeper had told them the way, and they stopped at Eboracum, going on from Eboracum to Bravoniacum. 'We're getting on nicely,' said Asterix. 'But it's time we changed horses again. Everyone look out for a horse-hiring stables!'

Throw the special DICE to find out who sees the stables first.

If you throw ASTERIX	go to 212
If you throw OBELIX	go to 121
If you throw DOGMATIX	go to 135

181

'The password is *BARLEY*,' said Asterix, 'and we're in a hurry, so kindly don't waste any more of our time!' The Roman soldiers were so startled at being addressed in such confident tones by a couple of civilians that their jaws dropped. 'Pass, friends!' they said, and the Gauls strolled slowly by as if they hadn't a care in the world. Once out of sight of the Romans, however, they quickened their pace as they made for Anticlimax's village. ***Go to 209.***

Dogmatix led the way down to the busy harbour of Portus Itius. 'Look!' exclaimed Asterix. 'What luck! That's a ship from Tyre lying at anchor – and there's our friend Ekonomikrisis the Phoenician! He must have put in here for the summer sales! Everything should be plain sailing now.' But it wasn't – they found themselves confronted by a Roman official demanding money. 'We were only going to look at the ships in harbour,' said Asterix. 'You want money for that? It's extortion . . . let us by!' 'No, but I'll let you *buy*,' said the corrupt official, winking. 'That'll be four coins!'

Is OBELIX carrying a COINBAG? If so, count out four coins by rotating the disc, and go to the number shown on the other side. If not, go to 81.

'She says we must go on along Watling Street, and then we'll come to Viroconium, which is the right way to go for the island of Mona,' Obelix interpreted. The girl said something else, and handed them a piece of parchment. It was a map of Britain which she had stolen from her captors, hoping it might help her to escape some day, as she told them in sign language, but now she was generously giving it to the Gauls instead. They thanked her, wished her good luck, and drove on towards Viroconium.

If OBELIX is not already carrying the MAP, put it in his WAIST-SLIT. Now go to 38.

As the Gauls had no money, they decided they had better just force their way past the barrier. The alarmed toll-collector let out a yell, and a large force of Roman legionaries, armed to the teeth, came pounding out of the camp and down the road. Asterix decided he had better take some magic potion if he was going to help Obelix fight them off. 'You know,' he remarked to his friend, in mid-battle, 'even if we do get inside the camp of Chrysanthemum, we're never going to find out much at this rate. Fighting Romans may be fun, but it's no way to pick up secret information! Let's go somewhere a bit quieter and think what to do next.'

Remove a *MAGIC POTION CARD* from *ASTERIX'S WAIST-SLIT*. Now go to 50.

The sentries at the Tower of Londinium were much surprised when a huge Gaul marched straight up to them. 'Got any mistletoe in there?' asked Obelix, in his usual subtle fashion. 'Mistletoe?' said the guards, blankly. 'No, of course not! What do you think this is – the Winter Solstice decorations department of Harrodus, or something?' 'They say it's not in there,' Obelix told the others. 'Too bad,' said Asterix. 'Well, let's go on into the city of Londinium.' 'Look – there's one of those funny red double-decker chariots!' said

Obelix. 'Let's have a ride on it.' They went up to the top of the double-decker, and when the conductor came along, Asterix told him, 'We're Gauls on a sight-seeing tour of London. Er . . . one of the sights we specially wanted to see was some British mistletoe. We hear it's all been taken away to somewhere in the city here. I suppose you don't know where?' The chariot conductor started talking very excitedly, but in a broad Londinium dialect. 'It's what's called Cockney, I think,' said Asterix. 'I can't make it out at all. We need a translator!'

Is OBELIX carrying a TRANSLATOR? If so, use it to find out what the conductor is saying in the picture below, and follow the instruction given in the speech bubble. If not, go to 175.

186

'Now that Captain Oystus has told us to go ashore at Dubris, I remember the place from our last visit to Britain,' said Asterix, as the Gauls rowed towards some cliffs. 'There'll be bluebirds over the white cliffs of Dubris,' he sang to himself. 'Blue birds? I don't see any blue birds, only ordinary white seagulls,' said Obelix, baffled. 'You're right. It was just something that came into my head,' Asterix apologised. 'Anyway, this is no time for bird-watching.' ***Go to 172.***

Obelix got his way, and the Gauls set out to look for a good restaurant before they went any farther. '*Singularis porcus sanus in corpore sano*,' muttered Obelix, as they walked along. 'I beg your pardon?' said his startled friend. 'It's a bit of Latin I persuaded a Roman to teach me,' said Obelix. 'Well, he didn't have much choice, really. It means a healthy boar in a healthy body . . . at least, that's what I *think* it means. I don't see any restaurants specialising in boar on this road, do you?' 'I don't see any restaurants at all on this road,' said Asterix. In the end they felt so hungry that they knocked on the door of the nearest private house, and asked the Briton who opened it if he could give them a meal. 'I suppose so,' said the Briton, a rather surly character. 'There's a boar boiling in the pot.' 'Poor thing!' said Obelix, under his breath. 'Still, better than nothing.' 'And I'll want payment!' added the man. 'Five coins apiece – and another for the dog, if you want him to get anything to eat! That comes to eleven.'

Is OBELIX carrying a COINBAG? If so, count out the eleven coins by rotating the disc, and then go to the number shown on the other side. If not, go to 15.

By the time they had finished deciding that Obelix should approach the ancient Briton first, the old man had gone inside his hut and shut the door. Obelix went up to it and knocked . . . 'Oh, Obelix!' moaned his friend. 'How many times have I told you that a gentle tap is all that's needed when you knock at someone's door?' 'That *was* a gentle tap,' said Obelix, aggrieved. 'What's all this, eh, what? Who knocked my front door in, and who's going to pay for it?' demanded the furious Briton. 'He's got a point, you know,' said Asterix. 'We really ought to pay compensation for the door – how much will it cost to repair, sir?' he asked. Calming down, the Briton said it had cost fourteen coins when new. 'Have you got that much, Obelix?' asked Asterix.

Is OBELIX carrying a COINBAG? If so, count out fourteen coins by rotating the disc, and go to the number shown on the other side. If not, go to 28.

189

The steak-house manager was scowling angrily at the Gauls. 'I'm terribly sorry – we just haven't got the money,' said Asterix. 'If only we had time, we'd wash the dishes to pay for our meal.' Dogmatix showed his willingness to help by jumping up on the table and licking clean every dish in sight. For some reason, the steak-house manager didn't seem to like this, and scowled more angrily than ever. 'But we're in a hurry – look, this is genuine Gaulish magic potion!' said Asterix, giving him one of his precious gourds. 'It's worth much more than the price of our meal – take a drop and then try lifting that big oak table in one hand!' The manager tried the potion, and was surprised and delighted to find that it worked. He agreed that it was fair exchange for their dinner, and told them that if they were going to Caledonia, they should go on up the Fosse Way to Lindum.

*Remove a **MAGIC POTION CARD** from **ASTERIX'S WAIST-SLIT**. Now go to 180.*

190
'He's saying we're on course for the border of Caledonia, and it's marked by a great big Wall the Romans have built right across the country to keep out the Picts and Scots,' said Obelix, consulting his translator tablet. 'And he's warning us to look out for Romans watching the road just north of the town here!' 'Right – off we go!' said Asterix. *Go to 123.*

191
Obelix reached the mushrooms first. He picked and picked, collecting plenty to be taken back to Anticlimax's village, dried and stored. As the Gauls went on through the wood, looking for more mushrooms, they met a man in a pair of tartan trousers. He seemed to know who they were, since he went up to them, shook hands, and said something – the only trouble was, they couldn't make out a word of it except his name, which seemed to be McRobiotix. 'Judging by his trousers and that name, he must be a friend of McAnix, only he speaks a different Scottish dialect,' said Asterix. 'I expect he's on his way to join his allies in the village. I wonder what he's trying to tell us? If we had a translator, we could find out. Have you got one, Obelix?'

*Is **OBELIX** carrying a **TRANSLATOR?** If so, use it to find out* *what the Scot is saying in the picture below, and follow the instruction in the speech bubble. If not, go to 117 instead.*

'We'll look for somewhere outside Antirrhinum to hide, and see who's going in and out of the place,' said Asterix, as he, Obelix and Dogmatix went along the road towards the fortified Roman camp. However, when they reached Antirrhinum, there was no possible hiding place in sight. 'All right, we'll change our plans,' Asterix decided. 'Let's put on our innocent-tourist act!' The guard at the camp gates stared in astonishment as the Gauls informed him that they wanted to see round Antirrhinum. 'Nothing doing!' he said. 'You must be off your heads! No tourists in here, not unless they know the password – ha, ha, ha!'

Is OBELIX carrying a PASSWORD SCROLL? If so, find out the correct password by placing it exactly over the scroll shape on the next page – then follow the appropriate instruction. If not, you'll have to guess which instruction to follow.

```
A   R    E  N2  L M P

J   OKR     Z 9     8

A   UD I        I 9

        J A G G      L O

YE    R     D Y      P

  Z     L M     S

  G     W     T     R

L N E   R O S   S I

  P L U    N D     E
```

If you think it's BARLEY   go to 270
If you think it's OATS   go to 261
If you think it's WHEAT   go to 264

193

'What a nuisance!' said Asterix. 'No coinbag – and this man won't tell us the way for free!' 'Shall I shake him just a little?' said Obelix. 'No,' said Asterix. 'We may not like his mean ways, but shaking is only for Roman soldiers, remember? Look,' he told the man, 'we haven't got enough money, but I can pay with this valuable gourd of magic potion!' The Briton agreed to take it instead of the coins, and told the Gauls that if they went on to Deva, they would be heading in the right direction for Mona.

Remove a MAGIC POTION CARD from ASTERIX'S WAIST-SLIT. Now go to 153.

Obelix spotted an inn called the Chariot and Horses first. They sat down and ordered a meal. It was not a particularly good meal – boiled boar again, just as Obelix had feared – but at least it was something to fill the gap. 'And when I have a gap, it's a big gap,' said Obelix, with feeling. 'Like everything else about you – big, that's all I said!' added Asterix hastily, as Obelix started wondering whether to take offence. While they ate, the Gauls discussed their next move. 'Most of the orders to Roman troops are likely to come from Londinium,' said Asterix. 'So if we go that way, we're more likely to pick up useful information. Landlord! I see that three roads meet just outside this pub. Where do they go?' The landlord told them they led to Rutupiae, Durovernum and Durobrivae. 'We've been near at least one of those before, I think,' said Asterix, frowning, 'but I can't for the life of me say which is nearest Londinium! Have you got a map, Obelix?'

Is OBELIX carrying a MAP? If so, consult it to find which town is nearest Londinium, and follow the appropriate instruction. If not, you will have to guess which instruction to follow.

If you think it's DUROBRIVAE	go to 248
If you think it's DUROVERNUM	go to 60
If you think it's RUTUPIAE	go to 168

The Gauls rowed on and on along the south coast of Britain, and still there was no sign of Portus Adurni and the harbour called Portus Magnus. 'I think we must have made the wrong decision,' said Asterix. 'I don't remember this part of the coast at all from our last visit. I think we'd better turn round and make for Anderida.' When they were in sight of Anderida, however, they saw several Roman galleys anchored just offshore, and the quayside was milling with Roman legionaries. 'That doesn't look a good bet either,' said Asterix. 'Come on, let's try Dubris!' *Go to 172.*

'Wrong. The password is *not WHEAT*,' said the guards, looking very suspiciously indeed at the two Gauls. 'Just what are you doing here, so close to the little village this camp was built to watch?' Asterix did not think any explanation he could give would sound very convincing, and he didn't want to waste time now they were so close to Anticlimax's village. As the guards turned to summon reinforcements, he took some magic potion. 'Come on, Obelix! Let's barge our way through this camp and out the other side!' he said. 'Nothing I'd like better!' said Obelix happily, barging through just as Asterix suggested, and they made their way on towards Anticlimax's village.

Remove a *MAGIC POTION CARD* from *ASTERIX'S WAIST-SLIT. Now go to 209.*

As the Gauls set off along the road towards Corinium, the sun came out from behind some clouds. 'Wait a moment!' said Asterix, looking up at it. 'We seem to be going north-west, and that can't be right. I'm afraid we'll have to turn back – let's try Venta Belgarum.' When they reached Venta Belgarum, they thumbed a lift in a carrier's cart. The carrier knew all about Mykingdomforanos, and his brave resistance to the Romans. He passed the Gauls on to a second carrier, who passed them on to another, so that they got a lift all the way to the village. ***Go to 209.***

'Oh, all right, I see you know the password – yes, it's *THYME*, so I suppose it's dinner-thyme for you,' said the innkeeper, rather ungraciously. 'Boiled boar and mint sauce, that's all we've got on the menu today.' 'Or any other day, I bet,' muttered Obelix, disappointed in his hopes of a nice rare roast boar. He wasn't even surprised when the landlord slapped tankards of warm beer down in front of them to wash it down, and when Asterix asked for goat's milk instead, they were told, 'Goat's milk's off.' 'I dare say it is, too, in a place like this,' remarked Asterix. 'Well, at least this is basic nourishment, so eat up, Obelix, and then *we'll* be off.' ***Go to 228.***

'Let's try Ratae,' said Asterix. But when they reached the outskirts of Ratae, they decided they had better check, and went into a nearby sweet-shop. The friendly British shopkeeper said he was sorry, they had chosen the wrong way at the crossroads. 'You should have gone on along Watling Street – that's your best way to Mona,' he said. Talking to him, the Gauls failed to see a shifty-looking man slip out of the shop. 'Now where's *he* going?' the shopkeeper wondered out loud. 'That was Crosspax, that was – he's a real sourpuss, and not even my wares will sweeten him up. I sometimes suspect he collaborates with the Roman invaders!' Those suspicions proved to be well founded – for next moment a patrol of Roman soldiers appeared in the shop doorway. 'Aha!' said their leader. 'So the information we've just received was right! You're Asterix and Obelix, two notorious Gauls known to be on the loose in Britain!' 'And we're going to stay on the loose!' said Asterix, swigging some magic potion. Within a few moments he, Obelix and Dogmatix were out of the shop again, leaving the Romans flat on the floor, and driving their chariot away from Ratae towards Viroconium.

*Remove a **MAGIC POTION CARD** from **ASTERIX'S WAIST-SLIT**. Now go to 38.*

Boadicea was a tall, brave-looking woman with a lot of red hair. She welcomed the Gauls to her camp. 'We hope to go on south-east, to meet Chief Mykingdomforanos and his men!' she said. 'And now that you've helped your friends in Cantium, you say you're looking for mistletoe? I'm afraid I don't know much about mistletoe, but I do know Londinium's a dangerous place for anyone but Romans at the moment. You might do better to try Caledonia first. I know it's a long way, but I'll lend you a chariot.' 'Thank you very much, ma'am,' said Asterix. 'That will be a great help!' They set off in the borrowed chariot, and after some time they reached a town called Ratae. 'I'm ravenous,' said Obelix, and Asterix and Dogmatix agreed. 'Let's look for a restaurant,' said Asterix.

Throw the special DICE to decide who chooses the restaurant.

If you throw ASTERIX	go to 24
If you throw OBELIX	go to 13
If you throw DOGMATIX	go to 137

201

As the Gauls stood outside the cellar door, however, it opened and several Roman legionaries came out. 'No civilian personnel allowed!' said the decurion. 'There's a dangerous secret weapon in here, I'd have you know – confiscated from the British resistance movement!' 'By Toutatis, so there is!' said Asterix, seeing beautiful piles of green mistletoe with pearly white berries lying in the cellar behind the man. 'Er – that's all right,' he added. 'We're Gaulish agents sent by Caesar to take this secret weapon over the Mare Britannicum and back to Rome!' 'Are you, indeed?' said the decurion, sceptically. 'Then of course you know the password?'

Is OBELIX carrying a PASSWORD SCROLL? If so, use it to find the correct password by placing it exactly over the scroll shape below, and follow the appropriate instruction. If not, you must guess which instruction to follow.

```
D    O    N    A K
K  P    E    B    A B
R    Y    P R    V A
N    S    WI    N
K    L    E    L E
B    A    GU    M
  E  L  O  Y  L  I
  T  A  N  A    B
6 !    O    K O    V
```

If you think it's MISTLETOE	go to 80
If you think it's PARSLEY	go to 152
If you think it's THYME	go to 164

202

They got out the map of Britain and looked at it. 'By Toutatis!' said Asterix. 'Verulamium is the closest of those towns to Londinium, and it's only about a day's march away. If the reinforcements coming from there are on the way already, they'll soon be here, preparing to join the men stationed in Durobrivae barracks and attack Chief Mykingdomforanos. Quick – we must go back to the village and warn our friends without wasting any time!' *Go to 211.*

Asterix strolled up to the barracks entrance, whistling non-chalantly. 'I say, is this Durobrivae barracks?' he asked. 'This is a barracks. That town there is Durobrivae. Work it out for yourself!' said the sentry, sarcastically. Asterix was tempted to drink some magic potion and knock the sentry into the middle of next week, but he didn't. It would have been a waste of potion, and besides, it could hardly be called a subtle method of bluffing his way in. 'Very funny, I'm sure,' he said. 'I'm from the village of Linoleum in Gaul, where Chief Cassius Ceramix the well-known collaborator with the Romans lives. I've brought important messages from him for your commanding officer, Centurion . . . er, Centurion . . . now what *was* his name?' He tried to sound as if it had just slipped his memory for a moment. The sentry fell for his trick. 'Centurion Outrageous,' he said. 'That's right, Outrageous – same as Cassius Ceramix's conduct,' added Asterix, under his breath. Just at that moment Centurion Outrageous himself appeared. 'From Cassius Ceramix, did you say? Glad to hear it!' he unexpectedly remarked. 'The old skinflint owes me money from when I was stationed in Gaul. You've come to pay it back, I suppose? You'd better!' he added, menac-ingly. Asterix mentally cursed Cassius Ceramix for landing him in this unexpected complication. 'Nineteen coins,' said the centurion. 'I'll just see if my friend has it on him,' said Asterix.

Is OBELIX carrying a COINBAG? If so, count out nineteen coins by rotating the disc, and go to the number shown on the other side. If not, go to 204.

Obelix was not carrying a coinbag, and even if he had been, Asterix didn't see why they should be landed with Chief Cassius Ceramix's debts. 'I don't know what you're talking about!' he told Centurion Outrageous. 'Cassius Ceramix never mentioned those nineteen coins to me!' 'No, well, he didn't know I was in command of Durobrivae barracks, did he?' said Centurion Outrageous, grinning. 'Right, I'm keeping you two as hostages until Cassius Ceramix pays up – you can kick your heels in the cells here while I send a message off to Linoleum!' This was terrible – not only would Ceramix certainly refuse to ransom Asterix, but the wait would hold up the whole of Operation Britain! As Centurion Outrageous was summoning men to seize the Gauls, there was nothing for it: Asterix had to drink a magic potion. There was a brisk little battle. 'You know,' said Asterix, surveying the flattened Roman legionaries, 'I don't know that we'll be very welcome inside the barracks after this. In the circumstances we'd better go round outside the fence and see what we can discover.'

*Remove a **MAGIC POTION CARD** from **ASTERIX'S WAIST-SLIT**. Now go to 11.*

As Obelix was not carrying a translator, the Gauls couldn't tell what the Britons outside the Dog and Dux were trying to say. Dogmatix had already dashed through the door, so Asterix and Obelix had to follow him. They rather wished they hadn't when, a moment later, a Roman patrol marched in – not that they minded tackling Romans, but it would have been better to get to Anticlimax's village unobserved. 'Two Gauls out on the town after curfew, eh?' said the decurion commanding the patrol. 'Er – no, sir!' said the friendly-looking landlord. Dogmatix had jumped up on the bar, hoping for a bowl of water. 'No, this little dog is the pub mascot,' the landlord went on, 'and these gentlemen are two of my regulars!' 'A likely story!' said the decurion. 'You're all coming with us – and so's the dog!' Asterix took a dose of magic potion – and between them, he, Obelix and Dogmatix efficiently flattened the Roman legionaries. 'Good show!' said the landlord. 'You'd better not be found here when their friends turn up, though. Try the Queen Boadicea just along the road – Beeswax the landlord is a friend of mine! He'll give you shelter for the night.'

Remove a MAGIC POTION CARD from ASTERIX'S WAIST-SLIT. Now go to 42.

206

'Yes, I'm off to Britain to pick up tin from the mines in the west, and sell the locals my incense, Tyrian purple, spices, precious stones . . . can I interest you gentlemen in anything?' asked Ekonomikrisis, as his ship drew out of harbour flying a flag advertising UNREPEATABLE OFFERS. 'No? Well, never mind, I can drop you off anywhere along the south coast of Britain.' But about halfway over the Mare Britannicum, a large Roman ship barred the Phoenician vessel's way. Its captain hailed Ekonomikrisis. 'Captain Nautilus, Roman Navy, commanding a patrol ship! Kindly state the nature of your business in these waters!' Ekonomikrisis looked alarmed, but Asterix told him, 'Don't worry! We'll deal with this for you – it's the least we can do in return for our passage.' All three of them were keen to help their old friend – even Dogmatix barked to show his willingness – so they drew lots to decide who would speak up for the Phoenician.

Throw the special DICE to find out who speaks to the Roman sea captain.

If you throw ASTERIX	go to 246
If you throw OBELIX	go to 227
If you throw DOGMATIX	go to 247

'Wrong. The password is not *BEER!*' said the decurion. 'Men, seize these two suspects – and the dog!' he added, as Dogmatix snapped at the legionaries' ankles. But the landlord of the Boar and Whistle must have been watching this scene, for he flung open the door of his pub again and created a diversion. 'Evening, decurion, sir! I was closed down right on time, as you can see – but let me make an exception for your good self and your men! Come along in and have a free meal!' 'A free meal of what?' asked the decurion. 'Boiled boar and mint sauce – delicious! With plenty of warm beer to wash it down!' said the landlord, temptingly. 'Boiled boar – yuk! Warm beer – yukkier!' gasped the decurion, flinching and turning pale. His men flinched too – and the Gauls seized their chance to get away, run down the road, and in through the door of the Queen Boadicea. 'I'm Beeswax,' said the landlord of the Queen Boadicea, shutting it behind them. 'Aren't you two indomitable Gauls from across the Channel, what? Pleased to meet you! You'll be quite safe for the night here.' *Go to 42.*

208

Obelix saw a sign saying CHARIOTS FOR HIRE first. They went in to hire a chariot and pair, and soon they were bowling merrily along Watling Street. When they had gone some way, they came to a place where another big Roman road called the Fosse Way joined it, and there was a signpost pointing three ways. One said Ratae, the second Viroconium, and the third Glevum. 'I wonder which of those towns is closest to Mona?' said Asterix. 'If we could be sure of that we'd know which road to take.'

Is OBELIX carrying a MAP? If so, consult it to find out which town is nearest to Mona and follow the appropriate instruction. If not, you'll have to guess which instruction to follow.

If you think it's GLEVUM	go to 280
If you think it's RATAE	go to 199
If you think it's VIROCONIUM	go to 156

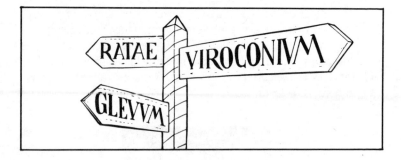

209

At last the Gauls had reached Anticlimax's village. Their old friends welcomed them warmly. The fresh supplies of tea Getafix had sent were very welcome too. That evening, Chief Mykingdomforanos held a council in his house, over a really strong brew of the potion that gave the Britons *almost* superhuman strength. 'Yes,' he told Asterix and Obelix, 'the magic mistletoe grows in those three oak-woods – one on the borders of Caledonia, one on the island of Mona, one near Londinium. I wish one of us could go with you, as a guide, but we need every man we have here! The Romans have built three fortified camps just outside the village, called Delphinium, Antirrhinum and Chrysanthemum, and it looks as if they're about to launch a concerted attack on us.' 'We don't need a guide,' said Asterix, 'I'm sure we can find our own way. But anything you can tell us about the situation in Britain will be useful – and before we leave, we'll help you deal with the Romans who threaten to attack you!' 'Will you really?' said Mykingdomforanos. 'I tell you what,

what!' said Anticlimax. 'If you went scouting round the camps you might pick up some useful information. The Romans know all of us by sight now – but they might not recognise you two and Dogmatix.' 'Good idea,' said Asterix. 'We'll start by trying to ask some questions – bluff sometimes works well.' So next day the Gauls and Dogmatix prepared to set out on their scouting expedition. 'Which camp shall we try?' said Asterix. It turned out that he favoured Antirrhinum, Obelix wanted to go to Delphinium, and Dogmatix kept starting off towards Chrysanthemum.

Throw the special DICE to decide whose choice of camp they visit first.

If you throw ASTERIX	go to 240
If you throw OBELIX	go to 63
If you throw DOGMATIX	go to 140

210

The Gauls had no coinbag – and Obelix did not like the British peasant's mercenary attitude. He looked very menacing as he stretched out a huge paw to pick the man up and shake him. 'Eek!' squeaked the peasant, in alarm, but he rather bravely added, 'Pick somebody your own size, can't you?' 'Quite right!' said Asterix. 'Leave him alone, Obelix! *I'll* fight you for the information,' he offered. 'Come on then, titch!' said the man, little knowing that the stuff he had just seen Asterix drinking was magic potion. The fight was all over in two seconds flat. 'I give in!' gasped the man. 'Yes, Queen Boadicea led a revolt against the Romans – sacked Camulodunum – and if you go to the camp of Antirrhinum you might find out more. The legionaries from the Camulodunum action retreated there.'

Remove a MAGIC POTION CARD from ASTERIX'S WAIST-SLIT. Now go to 192.

211

Asterix, Obelix and Dogmatix were soon back in the little village in Cantium with their news, so the Britons were ready and waiting for the Romans who came marching up from Durobrivae barracks and the camps of Antirrhinum, Delphinium and Chrysanthemum next morning. 'A good day's fighting!' said Chief Mykingdomforanos, with satisfaction, as they all leaned over the village fence watching the Romans carry out that famous military manoeuvre, the retreat in disorder. 'And it's just five o'clock, so now for a nice cup of tea!' Over a good strong brew in the chief's house, the Britons thanked Asterix and Obelix for all their help. 'That's quite all right,' said Asterix. 'Only too glad to be of use! Well, we'll set off on our own quest tomorrow – what do you Britons know about the oak-woods where the special magic mistletoe grows?' 'Not much more than Getafix told you,' said Anticlimax. 'British druids have always grown their mistletoe in Mona, and near the borders of Caledonia, and in the wood near Londinium.' 'I wonder which we should try first? I favour Londinium – it's the closest,' said Asterix. 'I wouldn't mind going to Caledonia,' said Obelix. 'I've always fancied a pair of those tartan trousers they make there.' Dogmatix started barking for all he was worth. 'I think he's saying *he* wants to try Mona, just to be different,' said Asterix, laughing.

Throw the special DICE to see who decides which oak-wood to make for.

If you throw ASTERIX	go to 276
If you throw OBELIX	go to 98
If you throw DOGMATIX	go to 118

212

Asterix was the first to see a stables with a sign outside saying HORSES FOR HIRE. Boadicea's chariot had needed several changes of horses on the way to Caledonia, and the Gauls had noticed that hiring horses cost more the farther north they went. 'I suppose it's just that there aren't so many horses up here,' said Asterix. He asked the proprietor of the stables how much a fresh change of horses would cost this time, and it was the most expensive yet. 'Thirteen coins!' said the man. Asterix's face fell. 'Can we afford it, Obelix?' he asked.

Is OBELIX carrying a COINBAG? If so, count out the thirteen coins by rotating the disc, and then go to the number shown on the other side. If not, go to 257.

213

'Well, let's try Corstopitum,' said Asterix. 'Cor, stop what?' asked Obelix. 'It. Um,' said Asterix. 'Never mind the silly jokes – there's no time to waste.' But halfway to Corstopitum, a breathless messenger on horseback overtook them. 'I've been sent by the Caledonian druids, who heard of your mission,' he said. 'I'm to warn you that all their mistletoe has been confiscated and taken to Londinium – the Romans must have heard, through their spies, who you were and where you were going. The druids too are fending off a Roman attack!' Dismayed, the Gauls realised they must go south to Londinium as fast as they could. 'But take this gourd of magic potion back to the Caledonian druids!' Asterix told the messenger. 'It may help them in their struggle against the Romans.'

Remove a MAGIC POTION CARD from ASTERIX'S WAIST-SLIT. Now go to 115. (Remember: when there are no magic potion cards left in Asterix's waist-slit Operation Britain cannot go on, and you must start the game again.)

214

Turning north meant a bit of extra rowing, but it also meant that the Gauls didn't set eyes on a single Roman ship as they crossed the Channel to Britain. Obelix was rather disappointed, but Asterix told him to cheer up. 'I'm sure we'll get plenty of excitement soon,' he said, as they sighted land. 'Now then, I wonder which is the nearest port to my cousin Anticlimax's village? We want to go there first, to find out the lie of the land. I remember hearing Anticlimax mention the ports of Dubris, Anderida and Portus Adurni – have you by any chance got a map on you, Obelix?'

Is OBELIX carrying a MAP? If so, consult it to see which port is nearest to Anticlimax's village, and follow the appropriate instruction. If not, you must guess which instruction to follow.

If you think it's ANDERIDA go to 90
If you think it's DUBRIS go to 225
If you think it's PORTUS ADURNI go to 195

'So you *don't* know the password. You were only guessing *OATS*!'
said one of the guards. 'What do we do now?' he asked his partner.
Both guards happened to be new recruits, and they were not quite
sure of procedure when someone couldn't answer their challenge.
Dogmatix showed what an intelligent dog he was by starting to bark
madly, and scrabbling at the ground as if he wanted to dig
something up. 'I say, do you think he's found buried treasure?'
Asterix asked Obelix, in a very loud voice. 'Dogmatix has always
had a good nose for buried treasure!' The two recruits, forgetting all
about their military duty, left their posts and went to investigate the
hole Dogmatix had begun to dig, whereupon the clever little dog left
it and ran off after the Gauls along the road leading to the village. *Go
to 209.*

'Er . . . the password's *GOAT*,' said Asterix, guessing. 'No, it
isn't,' said the decurion. 'Sorry, you'll have to turn back. You can't
go any farther without the password.' 'Can't we, though?' said
Obelix, who did not like anyone but Asterix telling him what to do.
Seizing the reins and uttering a loud Gaulish warcry, he made the
chariot swerve aside. His shout so terrified the two horses that they
raced away for dear life, right round the roadblock, leaving the
Roman soldiers staring after the chariot as it disappeared over the
horizon. By the time Asterix had managed to grab the reins back
from Obelix and calm the horses down, the Romans were out of
sight, and the Gauls went on their way to Viroconium. *Go to 38.*

It was decided that Dogmatix, who could look very appealing when he tried, should approach the peasant first, with a view to softening his heart. He went up to the man, sat down in the road, gazed at him with big, liquid eyes, and thumped his tail on the ground. Obviously the peasant's heart *was* softened, because he patted the little dog on the head and started talking to him – though unfortunately in a British dialect which Asterix and Obelix could not understand. When *they* spoke to *him*, asking if he had any information about Queen Boadicea, he seemed to understand the question, but they still couldn't make anything of his answer. 'Have you got a translator, Obelix!' asked Asterix. 'That might help us understand!'

Is OBELIX carrying a TRANSLATOR? If so, use it to find out what the man is saying and follow the direction given in his speech bubble below. If not, go to 113.

'They've raised the alarm!' exclaimed Asterix. 'Oh, what does that matter? We can cope with a few Roman soldiers!' said Obelix. 'No, wait – I'm afraid it's trickier than that,' said Asterix. For listening to the noises up above, they could make out the voices of Chief Mykingdomforanos and Queen Boadicea. 'Our allies – they've been taken prisoner!' cried Asterix. 'What do we do now?' said Obelix. 'We could always take some of this mistletoe and make a dash for it,' said Asterix, 'but that wouldn't be honourable! We must help our friends, and I'm afraid there are too many Romans up there for us to do it entirely on our own. Besides, I'm running short of magic potion. So first we must get out of the palace – leave the mistletoe for now, Obelix! Carrying it would slow us down. I hear legionaries coming, and if we don't run for it we'll be surrounded . . . And now,' he said, a little later, as they made off through the streets of Londinium, 'I'm afraid we'll have to abandon Operation Britain for the time being, report back to Gaul and get whatever help we can in our village, and then set off to rescue Mykingdomforanos and Boadicea. Once we've done that, perhaps we can have another go at the mistletoe. It will keep quite well down in a cellar – so with luck we may yet be able to bring Getafix back the supplies he needs to make his magic potion.'

OPERATION BRITAIN has not succeeded – but the Gauls are sure to be back, looking for the magic mistletoe. When you start the game again, try choosing a different item for Obelix to set out with. Better luck next time!

'Password?' said Asterix. 'I'm sure we *did* know the password . . . let's see, wasn't it *STAG*?' 'No, it was not!' said the decurion at the roadblock. 'Sorry, but you'll have to turn back. I can't allow you to go on along Watling Street.' 'Oh dear, what a shame,' said Asterix, pretending to accept this decision. 'I must adjust the horses' bridles before we turn back, though.' But, as he did so, he quietly slipped the two horses the contents of one of his gourds of magic potion. 'Right – gee up there!' he said, jumping up into the chariot again, and turning the horses' heads towards the roadblock. They smashed right through it with the greatest of ease, taking the chariot with them, and leaving the astonished Romans far behind. 'Right!' said Asterix. 'On we go to Viroconium!'

Remove a MAGIC POTION CARD from ASTERIX'S WAIST-SLIT. Now go to 38.

220

'*CAESAR*!' said Asterix, giving the correct password. 'Oh, very well, I suppose you're here on legitimate business of some kind,' said the official, letting the Gauls pass. (Dogmatix already *had* passed, without waiting for permission.) Following him down the cellar steps, Asterix and Obelix found themselves confronting two closed doors. 'Let's try this one on the left,' said Asterix. **Go to 79.**

221

'*HADRIAN* is wrong,' said the official, but the Gauls took no notice, and ran on down the cellar steps. Behind them, however, they heard the Roman summoning aid – and a dozen legionaries came chasing down the steps too. 'Watch your back, Obelix!' shouted Asterix, swallowing some magic potion, and both Gauls turned to face the enemies pouring downstairs to meet them.

Legionary after legionary was sent flying. 'People usually fall down the stairs, but that lot managed to fall up them instead,' said Asterix, smiling, as he cleared the last man out of the way. 'Now, we seem to have two cellar doors here – let's try the one on the left.'

Remove a *MAGIC POTION CARD* from *ASTERIX'S WAIST-SLIT.* Now go to 79. (Remember: when there are no magic potion cards left in Asterix's waist-slit Operation Britain cannot go on, and you must start the game again.)

222

'It must have been Camulodunum!' said Asterix, looking at the map. 'That's not far from the east coast.' 'You're right – I remember it, now! Yes, Queen Boadicea sacked Camulodunum!' said the peasant. 'Did he get another job?' asked Obelix sympathetically. 'Camulodunum is a place, not a person,' Asterix explained. 'I expect she put it to fire and the sword?' 'Yes, fire and the sword it was,' agreed the peasant. 'By the way, there were Roman soldiers going along that road just now.' He pointed to the road he meant. 'If you hurry, you might catch them up and find out more!' 'If they went that way, I'd guess they're making for the fortified camp of Antirrhinum,' said Asterix. 'That's it – I heard one of them say so. They dropped this. You'd better take it with you and give it back to them – or not, as the case may be,' added the peasant, winking, as he handed the Gauls a bag of coins.

If *OBELIX* is not already carrying the *COINBAG*, put it in his *WAIST-SLIT.* Now go to 192.

They decided that Obelix should ask the way, and he went up to a man walking down the street. 'Yes, I can tell you the way to Mona!' he said. Then a crafty look came into his eye. 'Foreigners, aren't you? I suppose you can pay for the information?' 'Pay?' said Obelix. 'Most people will tell us the way for free.' 'Ah, but you're foreigners, aren't you?' said the man, sticking to his point. Neither Asterix nor Obelix could actually *see* the point, but they were in a hurry to reach the magic mistletoe. 'How much do you want?' asked Asterix. 'Sixteen coins,' said the man.

Is OBELIX carrying a COINBAG? If so, count out the sixteen coins by rotating the disc and go to the number shown on the other side. If not, go to 193.

Asterix tried asking the landlord of the inn where they had spent the night. 'Mona?' said the landlord. 'Well, I know you need to go north from Viroconium, but after that I'm not so sure – it may be Deva you want, or then again, it could be Mamucium or Danum.' 'Have we got a map?' asked Asterix. 'Then we could see which of those towns is nearest to Mona.'

Is OBELIX carrying a MAP? If so, use it to see which of the three towns is nearest to the island of Mona, and follow the appropriate instruction. If not, you must guess which one to follow.

If you think it's DANUM	go to 167
If you think it's DEVA	go to 40
If you think it's MAMUCIUM	go to 254

'Hullo – what's that?' wondered Asterix, as the Gauls rowed towards Dubris. 'Looks like a bit of flotsam. Put out an oar and fish it in, will you, Obelix?' The flotsam turned out to be a crate marked with the skull and crossbones. 'This must have been washed overboard from the pirate ship!' said Obelix. 'Look, it's got the pirates' packed lunch in it! Wild boar sandwiches – goody, goody! And a packed boar bone for Dogmatix. How thoughtful of the pirates.' Dogmatix, tackling the bone, barked to show he agreed. 'And there's something even more useful here too,' said Asterix, investigating. 'A translator tablet with a list of foreign words! That ought to come in useful! I bet the pirates are sorry they lost it.'

If OBELIX is not already carrying the TRANSLATOR, put it in his WAIST-SLIT. Now go to 172.

'He says the camp isn't open to visitors,' said Obelix. 'That's a shame – I'd have liked to see some Roman antiquities. Specially Roman helmets – you know what a good collection of Roman helmets I've got. I might have been able to add to it!' 'We're not here to add to your helmet collection, Obelix,' said Asterix patiently. 'We're here, first, to help our British friends, and then to find the mistletoe Getafix needs to brew the magic potion. Come on – we're not getting anywhere here! Let's go somewhere quiet, like that little wood, and decide what to do next.' *Go to 3.*

Obelix was delighted to be dealing with Captain Nautilus. This was just the kind of thing he had been hoping for . . . he boarded the Roman galley, informing the captain that their ship belonged to a friendly power, and shook him quite gently for a minute or so. All too soon, Nautilus caved in. 'Yes, of course you're friendly!' he gasped. 'Friendliest people I ever met, and do please put me down!' 'All right,' said Obelix, still giving him a little shake now and then, 'but suppose you tell us the names of some good places to land along the south coast of Britain first?' After hearing what Nautilus had to say, he leaned over the rail of the galley to tell the others, 'He says we could land at Anderida, or Portus Adurni, or near Isca.' 'If you've got a map, look and see which of those is nearest to Anticlimax's village – that's where we're going first,' said Asterix. 'Have you got one?'

Is OBELIX carrying a MAP? If so, see which of these places is nearest to Anticlimax's village and follow the appropriate instruction. If not, you will have to guess which instruction to follow.

If you think it's ANDERIDA   go to 69
If you think it's ISCA   go to 61
If you think it's PORTUS ADURNI   go to 56

After walking along for some time, the Gauls decided to stop for a rest. They turned off the road into a little woodland clearing. 'We ought to decide just what *kind* of useful information we're after,' said Asterix. 'For instance, we could try finding out about possible allies for Mykingdomforanos and the rest of our friends in their struggle against the Romans. I've heard Queen Boadicea mentioned once or twice since we arrived in Britain . . . let's see what else we can learn about her. Have you had a good rest now? Then let's go on and ask the first peasant we meet.' And soon they saw one coming down a lane towards the road.

Throw the special DICE to decide who will approach the British peasant.

If you throw ASTERIX	go to 143
If you throw OBELIX	go to 125
If you throw DOGMATIX	go to 217

It was no use – they couldn't understand what the British agent was saying. Fishcax sighed. 'I ask you – what's the use of sending that poor sole to this plaice? All I can say is that I myself have seen Roman legionaries making for Chrysanthemum, so you could do worse than try there. And do take as much fish as you'd like!' 'Thank you,'

said Asterix. 'You've been very kind – the least we can do is offer you this gourd of magic potion in return, in case you or your contacts need it in an emergency some time!'

*Remove a **MAGIC POTION CARD** from **ASTERIX'S WAIST-SLIT**. Now go to 171.*

230

It was decided that Dogmatix should approach the ancient Briton first. Unfortunately, though he was a very friendly little dog, and frisked around very appealingly, he couldn't seem to make himself understood. So Asterix went up to the ancient Briton and tried asking the way – but he found that *he* couldn't get very far either. It seemed as if the Briton could understand, but spoke a British dialect which the Gauls didn't know. 'Have you got a translator, Obelix?' asked Asterix. 'That might help!'

*Is **OBELIX** carrying a **TRANSLATOR**? If so, use it to find out what the Briton is saying, and follow the instruction in the speech bubble. If not, go to 244.*

Asterix went up to the Roman soldiers guarding the entrance to the Tower of Londinium. 'We're innocent Gaulish tourists on a sight-seeing expedition,' he told them. 'When is the Tower open?' 'Never! This is a high-security Tower!' said one of the sentries. 'No tourists allowed in – you'd have to know the password, and that's not likely!'

Is OBELIX carrying a PASSWORD SCROLL? If so, find out the correct password by placing it exactly over the scroll shape below, and follow the appropriate instruction. If not, you must guess which instruction to follow.

```
    P   L    A      N
        T      EZW
    U      N    SA
       UL        E
    A    UIC        I
      M    ET       I
       NER     ES A
    P     A   LE   U
    R    M    E    N    E
```

If you think it's BEER	go to 150
If you think it's MEAD	go to 104
If you think it's WINE	go to 12

Dogmatix went up to the fishmonger first, wagging his tail. 'A dog, asking for fish?' said the astonished Fishcax. 'Cats, yes, but I didn't know dogs liked fish.' 'Dogmatix is a very special dog,' said Obelix. Asterix agreed, and quickly told the fishmonger who they were, and what their mission was. 'I wish I could tell you more,' said Fishcax. 'One of our spies in the resistance is here, in fact, and *he* could probably help you. The only trouble is that he comes from a part of Britain whose dialect even I don't understand! Flapjax!' he called, and a Briton emerged from the back of the shop. But it was quite true – the Gauls couldn't make out what he was telling them.

Is OBELIX carrying a TRANSLATOR? If so, find out what the Briton is telling him in the speech bubble below, and go to the number given there. If not, go to 229.

'I'm afraid we can't afford your entrance fee,' said Asterix. 'I tell you what, though,' he added, seeing the disappointment on Obelix's face, 'why don't we do a spot of dolmen-shifting for you – tidy the place up a bit, that kind of thing, and then maybe you'd let us look round?' The druid, looking at the sheer size of Obelix, agreed – and was much surprised when Asterix, tossing back a magic potion, proved as good at moving dolmens as his huge friend. With both of them at work, there was still time for a guided tour of Stonehenge before night fell. The grateful druid also gave them directions for reaching a place where they could spend the night.

Remove a MAGIC POTION CARD from ASTERIX'S WAIST-SLIT. Now go to 109.

234

The Gauls hadn't enough money for a good meal and a night's lodging at the Queen Boadicea. 'What a shame – it looks a nice place,' said Asterix. 'Still, we'll have to look for somewhere cheaper.' Just then a Roman patrol came marching down the street and in through the door of the pub. 'Now then, Beeswax!' said the decurion leading it. 'Let's have a look in your cellar – just to check you're not storing any smuggled Gaulish wine down there!' 'Here, I say!' protested the landlord indignantly. 'An Englishman's pub is his castle, don't you know, what! I know *your* way of checking – it leaves my cellar empty!' 'Too bad!' said the decurion, grinning. 'Come on, we can't have this!' whispered Asterix, swallowing some magic potion, and he and Obelix fell on the astonished patrol. The scuffle was short and sharp – particularly sharp when Dogmatix used his teeth. 'Thanks!' said the grateful Beeswax, when the Romans had been thrown out. 'I say – don't I recognise you? Surely you're Asterix and Obelix, our famous Gaulish allies! Come in! You can spend the night here free, and there's a roast boar on the spit!'

Remove a MAGIC POTION CARD from ASTERIX'S WAIST-SLIT. Now go to 42.

'So here it is at last!' said Asterix happily. 'Lots and lots of wonderful magic mistletoe, just what the druid ordered.' Quickly, he and Obelix picked up some sacks and began stuffing mistletoe into it. Dogmatix helped, carrying the best sprays over to them in his mouth. 'And now,' said Asterix, 'we'll go out of the Governor's palace by the back door, and get back to Anticlimax's village. We can go home to Gaul from there!' They had no trouble in returning to the wood where they had left their chariot, and driving the mistletoe back to Cantium, where Mykingdomforanos, Anticlimax and their friends were delighted to see them. It so happened that Ekonomikrisis put in at Dubris next day, and gave the heroes a lift back to Gaul. Back in the Gaulish village, everyone was delighted to see them, particularly Getafix, who set about brewing fresh supplies of magic potion straight away. A banquet was held to celebrate their return, with all the roast boar Obelix wanted. The only awkward moment was when Cacofonix rose to try out the Caledonian bagpipes his friends had rashly brought back for him, but he was quickly gagged, bound and parked under a tree – as everyone agreed that Cacofonix playing the bagpipes really would be **THE END**.

You have completed OPERATION BRITAIN successfully and finished the game!

'*CLAUDIUS*?' said Asterix, guessing. 'Wrong!' said the official. 'So get out, and take that nasty dog of yours with you!' He even aimed a kick at Dogmatix. Asterix was so infuriated by this behaviour that he decided the Roman needed to be taught a lesson. 'Take that!' he said, slamming the official into the ceiling high above. 'And I hope it teaches you to be kind to animals in future! Now then, I wonder which of these doors has mistletoe behind it?' he said, joining Dogmatix and Obelix at the bottom of the cellar steps. 'Let's try the one on the left.'

Remove a *MAGIC POTION CARD* from *ASTERIX'S WAIST-SLIT*. Now go to 79. (Remember: when there are no magic potion cards left in Asterix's waist-slit Operation Britain cannot go on, and you must start the game again.)

Dogmatix was so eager to go down *his* road that Asterix and Obelix humoured him. However, they soon discovered that the great attraction was a butcher's shop just round the corner. The kindly butcher, seeing a nice little dog looking longingly into his window, gave Dogmatix a bone – but when the Gauls tried asking him the way to Anticlimax's village near Cantium, they couldn't understand him. 'He doesn't speak like the Britons we've met before, though he seems to understand *us* all right,' said Asterix. 'Bother! What we need is a translator tablet, Obelix – have you got one on you?'

Is OBELIX carrying a TRANSLATOR? If so, use it to find out what the butcher is saying in the picture below, and follow the instruction given in the speech bubble. If not, go to 277.

Hoping for the best, Asterix made a guess at the password. 'Ho, ho, ho!' said the decurion, chuckling. '*BARLEY*, did you say? Wrong! You're coming back to HQ with us to explain yourselves to the centurion!' Asterix thought quickly. 'Hey, look!' he shouted, pointing to some military equipment being unloaded on the quayside. 'That battering ram's come adrift!' And as the decurion and his men swung round to look, all three dashed down to the beach. They soon saw a sign saying AQUATIX: JOLLY-BOATS FOR HIRE. Aquatix, recognising the famous Asterix and Obelix, picked them his very best boat. *Go to 51.*

'They're warning us that the Romans are clamping down on closing-time in British pubs, and we must be careful if we don't want to be picked up for being out and about after curfew,' said Obelix. The Britons all started talking again, pointing down the road. The words 'Queen Boadicea' could be heard, several times. 'That's the name of the first inn we saw,' said Asterix. 'I think they're advising us to go there!' Sure enough, when they reached it, the landlord, Beeswax, welcomed them. 'You're Gaulish allies of our brave men in the village in Cantium, aren't you?' he said. 'I'm in the British resistance – you'll be safe here for the night!' *Go to 42.*

The Gauls slipped quietly out of the British village, but once they felt sure no one had seen them leaving it, they strode boldly up to the fortified Roman camp at Antirrhinum. 'Now, what story can we tell?' Asterix wondered. 'We don't need a story, do we?' said Obelix. 'We'd like to come in and look around,' he told the guard at the gate. 'I wish,' said Asterix, under his breath, 'I *do* sometimes wish you could be a little more subtle, Obelix!' '*Look around*!' gasped the guard. 'Er . . . that's right!' said Asterix, making the best of it. 'We're tourists, you see. Tourists from Gaul, come to see the sights of Britain, and naturally we want to look round one of your famous fortified Roman camps!' 'But – but you can't come into a fortified Roman camp, just like that!' said the astonished guard. 'Not unless you know the password, that is!'

Is OBELIX carrying a PASSWORD SCROLL? If so, use it to find out the correct password by placing it exactly over the scroll shape below. Then follow the appropriate instruction. If not, you must guess which instruction to follow.

```
   P   L   A   N
       T     E Z W
  U        N    S A
     U L         E
  A    U I C        I
  M     E T        I
    N E R      E S  A
  P   A     L E    U
  R   M E      N     E
```

If you think it's BEER	go to 159
If you think it's MEAD	go to 256
If you think it's WINE	go to 251

Dogmatix happily led the way to the Dog and Dux. 'I wonder if he thinks it's an inn specially *for* dogs?' said Asterix, as he and Obelix followed. But they hesitated before going in. There were several Britons standing outside, talking excitedly to each other in an obscure British dialect the Gauls didn't understand. Spotting Asterix and Obelix, they spoke to them. 'They seem to be trying to tell us something,' said Asterix. 'I wonder what it is? Do you have a translator on you, Obelix?'

Is OBELIX carrying a TRANSLATOR? If so, use it to find out what the Briton in the picture below is saying and follow the instruction. If not, go to 205.

They started out towards Lindinis, and soon they came to a river. As they stood wondering how to get across it, a boat came downstream – rowed by a nasty-looking character whose passenger, a very pretty girl, was bound and gagged. She made frantic, muffled attempts to call for help as she saw the two Gauls and the dog on the bank. 'By Toutatis, that man must have kidnapped her!' exclaimed Asterix. Swallowing some magic potion, he jumped into the river, picked the girl up, threw her to the bank, where Obelix caught her, and sent her kidnapper sailing up into the air. Nobody saw just where he came down, but it must have been a long way off. 'Oh, thank goodness!' cried the girl, when she had been freed from her bonds. 'That wicked man was going to ask my father for a huge ransom! How can we ever thank you?' 'Well, you could tell us if we're going the right way for Cantium,' said Asterix, as Obelix stared dreamily at the beautiful girl. 'I'm afraid not,' she said, 'but come back to my village with me, and my father, the village chieftain, will lend you a fast chariot to take you wherever you want to go.'

Remove a MAGIC POTION CARD from ASTERIX'S WAIST-SLIT. Now go to 209.

'Caught you out!' said Armisurplus. 'Ratae is nowhere near Caledonia, as you'd know if you were really on an innocent sight-seeing expedition. Seize those men!' he told his legionaries. Asterix quickly drank some magic potion, and between them he and Obelix sent Armisurplus and his men flying in all directions. 'If all these extra troops are arriving,' said Asterix, panting only very slightly as he and Obelix strolled away, 'it must mean that the attack is planned for some time very soon – I shouldn't be surprised if it was tomorrow. We must get back and warn the chief!'

Remove a *MAGIC POTION CARD* from *ASTERIX'S WAIST-SLIT*. *Now go to 211.*

But Obelix had no translator with him, and after a while the ancient Briton, though he was full of friendly smiles, gave up his attempt to make the two Gauls understand him. However, he kept pointing in one particular direction, and when Asterix asked, 'That way?' he nodded hard. He even mimed going to sleep, and drew the outline of a little hut on the earth of his flower-bed. 'He seems to be telling us that we shall find shelter for the night in a hut along the way,' said Asterix. They thanked the ancient Briton and set off the way he had been pointing. ***Go to 149.***

'The password is *MEAD*!' said Asterix. With several Britons watching the scene, the decurion couldn't deny that the two Gauls *had* given the correct password, and they went on down the street. 'Psst!' said a voice from a doorway. 'Quick – in here!' And they found themselves inside the Queen Boadicea inn, with the door locked after them. 'My name's Beeswax – I'm the landlord here!' said the Briton who had asked them in. 'Aren't you Asterix, Anticlimax's cousin once removed?' 'And his friend Obelix,' said Obelix. 'Jolly good show, what!' said Beeswax. 'You don't want to be out and about this time of night – too many Romans on the streets. You can stay the night here, for free.' *Go to 42.*

'This is a peaceful merchant vessel belonging to a friendly power,' Asterix told the Roman captain. Captain Nautilus did not look as if he believed this. 'Then what are you doing aboard her?' he asked.

'You look like a Gaul to me. In fact, you look like one of those indomitable Gauls from Armorica. You wouldn't be Asterix, would you?' 'Never heard of him!' said Asterix, cheerfully. 'I suppose you can give me the current password for all friendly trading vessels, can you?' said Captain Nautilus.

Is OBELIX carrying a PASSWORD SCROLL? If so, use it to find out the correct password by placing it over the scroll shape below and following the appropriate instruction. If not, you must guess which instruction to follow.

```
   D     O    N    A K
   K  P  E    B    A B
   R  Y  P R       V A
   N     S    W I  N
   K  L  E    L    E
   B     A    G U  M
      E  L  O  Y  L     I
   T  A     N    A      B
   6!    O    K O       V
```

If you think it's MISTLETOE	go to 176
If you think it's PARSLEY	go to 260
If you think it's THYME	go to 75

Dogmatix showed his willingness to deal with the Roman patrol ship by barking so furiously that Captain Nautilus, who did not like dogs at all, changed his mind about questioning Ekonomikrisis any further. 'It's all right!' he said hastily. 'Your ship can pass!' 'Well, you can give *us* some information!' said Asterix. 'My Phoenician friend here is going to sail along the south coast of Britain – tell us a good port for a large ship like his to put in!' 'I'm afraid I don't know – I'm new to these waters!' said Captain Nautilus, adding hastily, as Dogmatix opened his mouth to bark again, 'But one of my seamen knows Britain! He only speaks his own language, though. I can ask in sign language if you like.' The Gauls did like – but did they have a translator to help them understand the seaman's answer?

Is OBELIX carrying a TRANSLATOR? If so, find out what the seaman is saying in the picture below and follow the instructions in the speech bubble. If not, go to 278.

The Gauls paid for their meal. 'Cheer up, Obelix,' said Asterix, 'it was better than nothing! Now then, let's make for Durobrivae – that seems to be our best bet for trying to pick up any stray bits of information we can.' The road to Durobrivae was a good one, but it seemed as if it would be ages before it actually led them anywhere. *Go to 228.*

The Gauls had no translator tablet, so there was no way they could interpret the sentry's remarks, but he did not sound exactly welcoming. 'Never mind, let's just march in!' said Obelix, preparing to do just that. 'Obelix, no! You'll only draw attention to us!' Asterix shouted after him, but it was too late. Obelix was having a lovely time, punching Romans right, left and centre, and piling up their helmets one by one. 'Oh no!' groaned Asterix. 'How does he think we'll discover any useful information that way? I suppose I'll have to go in too,' he added, drinking some magic potion as he saw every soldier in the camp making for Obelix. So many Romans all at once might have been too much of a good thing, even for him, without Asterix to lend a hand. After an invigorating little punch-up, Asterix finally managed to get him away.

Remove a MAGIC POTION CARD from ASTERIX'S WAIST-SLIT. Now go to 50.

'It's LUGUVALLUM!' said Asterix, looking over Obelix's shoulder at the map. They drove towards Luguvallum, and asked the way to the oak-wood where the chief Caledonian druid lived. Even as they drove into the wood, however, they began to fear that something was wrong . . . there was not a bit of mistletoe to be seen growing on the trees. 'Alas, my friends,' exclaimed the chief Caledonian druid, 'you are too late!' Only a few days ago, Governor Encyclopaedicus Britannicus sent a party of soldiers to make us pick all our mistletoe, and they took it away to Londinium! They told me the Governor had sent men to seize the mistletoe from Mona, too.' 'Oh no – after we've come all this way!' exclaimed Asterix. 'Just as I suspected, the Romans have known about Operation Britain all

along! 'I suppose there's nothing for it – we'll have to go south again.'
'Good luck!' said the druid. 'And take this password scroll – it's all I
have to give you now.'

**If OBELIX is not already carrying the PASSWORD SCROLL,
put it in his WAIST-SLIT. Then go to 115.**

251

The guard at the camp gates looked even more astonished than
before when he found that the Gauls knew the correct password –
WINE. It wasn't usual to let civilians see inside military camps, but
he had to admit them in now. 'Er – well, look, here's Anonymus!' he
said, grabbing a passing friend of his. 'I'm sure he'll show you
round!' Anonymus looked even more astonished than the guard,
but he showed them round the inside of the camp all the same. In
fact, Asterix and Obelix saw nothing unusual in it. They had made
raids inside the fortified Roman camps around their own Gaulish
village often enough – but while Dogmatix created a diversion by
running off to see what was cooking over the legionaries' camp-fires,
Asterix took his chance to pick up a map of Britain which he saw
lying on the ground just outside a tent. 'Thank you for the guided
tour,' he said to Legionary Anonymus, and the Gauls went off,
making for a little wood.

**If OBELIX is not already carrying the MAP, put it in his
WAIST-SLIT. Then go to 3.**

'Well, upon my sole! Fancy meeting Anticlimax's cousin!' said Fishcax, beaming. 'Of course I believed you – but one can't be too careful these days.' '*MISTLETOE* is a password that suits us down to the ground,' said Asterix, and explained why. 'But before we go looking for the mistletoe our druid needs, we want to help Mykingdomforanos and his men against the Romans.' 'You were right about the Roman troops – they *are* on the move hereabouts,' said the fishmonger. 'That's as much as I know, though – why not try spying out one of the Roman camps, such as Chrysanthemum?' 'We didn't get very far with the Roman camps before, but it's worth another shot,' agreed Asterix. Fishcax gave him a huge basket of fish, refusing to let him pay, and then brought out something else. 'Here – it's a translator tablet. If you go to Chrysanthemum, you might find it useful.'

If OBELIX is not already carrying the TRANSLATOR, put it in his WAIST-SLIT. Now go to 171.

'Very interesting,' said Asterix, under his breath. 'So now we know there *have* been large forces landing in Britain, at Portus Adurni on the big harbour of Portus Magnus. Thank you very much!' he said out loud to the Briton. 'Nice little village you've got here – those Roman columns are the latest thing, aren't they?' 'That's right! I've got one in my own house,' said the Briton proudly. 'If you're interested in the magnificent army of our Roman allies, you might like to have this,' he added, giving the Gauls a password scroll. 'You'll find those newly arrived troops in the fortified camp of Delphinium – that's where they said they were going, and this could help you to get in.' 'It could indeed!' said Asterix, as Obelix pocketed the scroll.

If OBELIX is not already carrying the PASSWORD SCROLL, put it in his WAIST-SLIT. Now go to 160.

As they had no map, the Gauls had to guess which way to go, and they started out for Mamucium. Before they had gone very far, it began to pour with rain. 'Let's ask this carter if we're going the right way,' said Asterix, as they spotted a man coming towards them from Mamucium, in a cart. He warned them that Mamucium was famous for its rainy climate, but he said they were going the wrong way in any case. 'You want Deva,' he said. He looked so wet and miserable that Asterix rewarded him for his information with a gourd of magic potion to cheer him up, and turned the chariot back in the direction of Deva.

Remove a *MAGIC POTION CARD* from *ASTERIX'S WAIST-SLIT*. Now go to 153.

255

Asterix, Obelix and Dogmatix went on for some time before they saw houses ahead. 'A British village!' said Asterix. 'Let's go and see what they can tell us there!' said Obelix. 'Wait a moment, though,' said Asterix, looking more closely at the houses. 'See that? They've got quite a few Roman columns and such-like here . . . I wouldn't be surprised if this was a Romano-British settlement!' 'A what?' asked Obelix. 'Well . . . remember Chief Cassius Ceramix, back in Gaul?' said Asterix, trying to explain. 'He was collaborating with the Romans, and he got his villagers to build things in the Gallo-Roman style. Romano-British is the same thing, only in Britain. If you see what I mean.' 'Not really,' admitted Obelix. 'Well, what I really mean is watch your step!' said Asterix. 'Then why couldn't you say

so, instead of carrying on about Cassius Ceramix?' inquired the
bewildered Obelix, looking down at his feet. Then, however, they
saw a British villager. 'Let's go and talk to him,' said Asterix.

***Throw the special DICE to decide who speaks to the villager
first.***

If you throw ASTERIX	go to 21
If you throw OBELIX	go to 263
If you throw DOGMATIX	go to 58

256

'Wrong password! It's not *MEAD*,' said the guard at the gate.
'Here, Decurion Mountainus!' he asked an enormous man who
loomed up behind him. 'What do you make of this lot, saying
they're tourists who want to look round the camp?' 'Sinister,' said
Mountainus. 'Very sinister! You go and call the centurion,
Vociferus, and I'll keep an eye on them – and you can take that dog
as a hostage!' he added, suddenly grabbing Dogmatix and handing
him to Vociferus as the Gauls looked about to retreat. Obelix was not

having any of that! He flattened Vociferus and snatched Dogmatix back, while Asterix, taking a quick swig of magic potion, knocked the huge Decurion Mountainus right over the camp fence. Then the Gauls and Dogmatix ran for cover in a little wood.

*Remove a **MAGIC POTION CARD** from **ASTERIX'S WAIST-SLIT**. Now go to 3.*

257

Without a coinbag, Asterix did not see how they were going to pay for the change of horses they needed. 'Well,' he told Obelix, 'I've been keeping my potion for emergencies, and here's one of them. Look,' he said to the owner of the stables, 'have you ever heard of a magic potion brewed in Gaul by a druid called Getafix? Well, this is it!' 'My word!' breathed the man, much impressed. 'Will you take this gourd of potion as payment?' asked Asterix. 'I certainly will!' said the man. 'I've heard wonderful tales of that magic potion. Take the horses, and good luck! When you see a great big Wall, you'll know you're coming to the border of Caledonia.'

*Remove a **MAGIC POTION CARD** from **ASTERIX'S WAIST-SLIT**. Then go to 123.*

258

'He says that even in his obscure corner of Britain, they fear a new Roman offensive, and their fears are confirmed by what he's discovered today!' exclaimed Asterix, looking over Obelix's shoulder at the translation of what the Briton was saying. 'And he recommends us to go to the fortified camp of Chrysanthemum! That's more than useful – many thanks, Fishcax!' 'And have some fish to take with you!' said the friendly fishmonger. ***Go to 171.***

Asterix and Obelix took a quick look at the map they were carrying, which immediately told them the answer to Centurion Armisurplus's trick question. 'Habitancum, of course!' said Asterix. 'Told you we were innocent sight-seers, didn't we?' added Obelix. Dogmatix barked at the centurion. 'Any idea where we can see a good battle?' asked Asterix cheekily. Armisurplus was so surprised that he answered, 'Yes, at the rebel village holding out against us Romans, tomorrow!' 'Tomorrow? How interesting!' said Asterix, waving a cheerful goodbye as he and Obelix started off up the road to the village. *Go to 211.*

'Well, you seem to be telling the truth – you pass with *PARSLEY*,' said Captain Nautilus, sounding friendlier. 'That indomitable Gaulish look about you must be just a coincidence.' And as a gesture of goodwill, he gave the travellers a map of Britain before he ordered his men to row the patrol ship away. 'You keep it,' Ekonomikrisis told the Gauls. 'You can probably make good use of it. Now, suppose I drop you off at Anderida? We're nearly there now.'

If OBELIX is not already carrying the MAP, put it in his WAIST-SLIT. Then go to 132.

261

The guard was so startled to hear the Gauls give the correct password, *OATS*, that he just stood back and let them enter Antirrhinum. They wandered round, pretending to be staring in amazement at everything they saw – and they lingered outside a tent where two Roman officers were talking. 'So the attack's tomorrow, is it?' one was saying. 'That's right – as soon as the reinforcements from Verulamium arrive. Now that Boadicea has sacked Camulodunum, we want to get Chief Mykingdomforanos crushed before she comes any farther south. Those two leaders together would make a formidable team!' 'That's all we need to know!' Asterix whispered. 'Come on – we must tell Mykingdomforanos the news, quick!' **Go to 211.**

262

'Right, let's look for a little jolly-boat!' said Asterix, as they reached the harbour. 'We're sure to find some for hire down on the beach – come on!' Next moment, however, they found themselves facing a patrol of Roman legionaries commanded by a suspicious decurion. 'You can't go down to the harbour unless you know today's password!' he said.

Is OBELIX carrying a PASSWORD SCROLL? If so, use it to find the correct password by placing it exactly over the scroll shape below, and then follow the appropriate instruction. If not, you must guess which instruction to follow.

```
      S   P    S   P      H    R
   M O   L V S K       K  E
    N W Z              P H    L
   O    D C   X          Y
   4 K   E  B K        Z
     P E F      I       A
   J  H    V    X    Z 8
 Y Z  T   Q S         P B
    I Q T     M        Z
   A C I L      B      O
   P O D    K     D    Y
```

If you think it's BARLEY	go to 238
If you think it's OATS	go to 274
If you think it's WHEAT	go to 165

263

Obelix went up to the British villager first. He believed in the direct approach. 'Seen any good Romans lately?' he asked. 'Lots!' said the villager, briefly. 'Oh! Er . . . well, tell us about them, why don't you?' suggested Obelix. 'We're very interested in the Roman conquerors,' put in Asterix, truthfully enough. 'Specially the Roman army! Have you seen any newly landed troops passing?'

'We're not supposed to give information away. It's against Roman law. I've no objection to selling it, though,' said the Briton. 'The information you want will cost you five coins.'

Is OBELIX carrying the COINBAG? If so, count out the five coins by rotating the disc, and then go to the number shown on the other side. If not, go to 124.

264

'Wrong password – it isn't *WHEAT*!' said the guard. Obelix was all for breaking into the camp by force, but Asterix stopped him. 'We may be able to find out what we want to know by other means,' he said. 'Let's strike off across country.' They had not gone far across country when they came to a cottage on the outskirts of a wood. 'I'm thirsty,' said Asterix. 'I wonder if the people here could give us a drink of milk?' However, the Briton who lived there said he was sorry, they had no milk. 'In fact we haven't anything to eat or drink at all. A party of Roman soldiers came this way and took everything we had in the house!' he said. There were several children in the place, looking very hungry. 'Something must be done about this!' said Asterix, drinking some magic potion, and he and Obelix went off into the wood and came back with several boars for the family. The grateful Britons told them that they had heard the Romans who plundered them saying the rebel village was to be attacked next day. 'Then we must hurry back and give this information to Myking-domforanos! Thank you, and goodbye!' said Asterix, and they set off quickly.

Remove a MAGIC POTION CARD from ASTERIX'S WAIST-SLIT. Now go to 211.

'*HADRIAN* it is,' said the centurion, when the Gauls gave him the password. 'Well, I suppose you must have business up here in the north after all. What is it?' 'That's not fair, when we've given him the password,' Obelix grumbled. 'Why's he picking on us when he could have picked a Pict instead?' he went on. But Asterix was ready with a plausible story. 'We're Gauls loyal to Caesar, and we've come north from Londinium, with messages from Governor Encyclopaedicus Britannicus for the men garrisoning the Wall,' he said. 'The only trouble is,' he added, truthfully, 'travelling through Britain is so expensive we're running short of cash. Can you lend us some? The Governor will pay you back when you get to Londinium.' 'Certainly,' said the centurion, giving the Gauls a coinbag. 'Carry on north for the Wall.'

If OBELIX is not already carrying the COINBAG, put it in his WAIST-SLIT. Then go to 123.

'*RAM* is not the password, and I don't believe a word of your story!' snapped the centurion. 'Walking the dog, indeed! I'm taking you to Londinium for further questioning – you look like Gauls to me, and I've heard two dangerous Gauls are on the "Wanted" list!' Obelix moved forward to tackle the Romans, and when he looked at all the men disembarking on the river bank, Asterix realised there were more than even his immensely strong friend could be expected to deal with on his own. He drank one of his magic potions, and joined the fray. Between them, they had soon flattened enough of the disembarking men to send the others scurrying back on board their galley for safety. 'Come on!' gasped Asterix. 'Let's get out, quick! I think we should make for Durovernum.'

Remove a MAGIC POTION CARD from ASTERIX'S WAIST-SLIT. Now go to 72.

Just as Dogmatix was about to run down the cellar steps, a sour-faced official emerged from a door nearby. 'A dog?' he said. 'What's a dog doing in here, by Jupiter, leaving muddy footmarks all over the place? Here – you two! Is this dog yours? Can't you control him? And what are *you* doing in the palace anyway? No one's allowed in without giving the password – do you know it?'

Is OBELIX carrying a PASSWORD SCROLL? If so, find out the correct password by placing it exactly over the scroll shape below, and then follow the appropriate instruction. If not, you must guess which instruction to follow.

```
        B   RI   T      O
          C P      FS A    Z
        !   LM       S   G
          W R E   6      7
        F  A L  S     E   T
           A  T   O    PPI
        D   U M R      H   I
        C   H     AE    C
        A    H    OC   9!
```

If you think it's CAESAR	go to 220
If you think it's CLAUDIUS	go to 236
If you think it's HADRIAN	go to 221

268

Asterix started down the cellar steps, only to find his way barred by an enormous Roman soldier. 'And what do you think you're doing here?' asked the soldier. 'We're plumbers, come about the pipes,' said Asterix, but his excuse didn't work this time. 'No pipes down here,' the soldier told him. 'The place is stuffed with mistletoe, that's all!' Asterix was delighted to hear it. 'Mistletoe! That's wonderful!' he said. 'I mean – I mean we're not *just* plumbers, we're plumbers on a sight-seeing tour, and one of the things we'd simply love to see is some mistletoe!' 'There's something funny about you, though I can't quite work out what,' said the Roman soldier, who was rather stupid. He was also very greedy. 'But slip me fifteen coins, and I'll let you go down!' he added.

Is OBELIX carrying a COINBAG? If so, count out the fifteen coins by rotating the disc, and go to the number shown on the other side. If not, go to 114.

269

'What made you say *HADRIAN*?' inquired the decurion in charge of the roadblock. 'It's wrong – but you're not by any chance friendly with those Picts and Scots, are you?' 'Er – no, no, not a bit of it!' said Asterix hastily. 'I always thought Chief McAnix was rather a good sort!' objected Obelix. 'Shut up!' his friend hissed, turning back to the decurion. 'It's funny you should mention Picts and Scots,' he said innocently, 'because I'm sure we saw some lurking in the bushes as we came up the road just now. Over there!' And he pointed. 'What? Where? Come on, men!' shouted the decurion – and as the legionaries went haring off down the road the Gauls made their way past the roadblock. 'Fancy thinking he'd find Scots this far south!' Asterix chuckled. 'Let's go on a bit and then look for a friendly British house where we can spend the night.' **Go to 109.**

270

'*BARLEY*, indeed!' said the guard at the camp gates, sarcastically. 'You haven't got a hope of getting inside Antirrhinum. Take yourselves off!' 'No – *you* try taking off!' said Asterix, drinking some magic potion and sending him flying up in the air. Obelix was already well inside the camp. 'You needn't bother to come in, Asterix,' he called back. 'I've already persuaded this nice Roman to tell us what we want to know – the village is going to be attacked tomorrow!' He dropped the Roman he had been shaking, and the man sent flying by Asterix came down to earth too, as the two Gauls started up the road to Anticlimax's village.

Remove a MAGIC POTION CARD from ASTERIX'S WAIST-SLIT. Now go to 211.

271

'So to get to Caledonia, we want to go on up the Fosse Way from Ratae to Lindum,' said Asterix, looking over Obelix's shoulder at the translator. The waiter from Hispania burst into another flood of excited remarks. 'And he seems to be warning us about something called porridge. Well, we'll face that additional peril when we come to it. Let's hire fresh horses for Boadicea's chariot, and drive on to Lindum.' *Go to 180.*

272

They couldn't understand what the slave-girl was saying, but as she kept pointing straight ahead, they worked out that they must still be going the right way. 'You know, I feel so sorry for her, I don't think I should keep the magic potion to myself,' said Asterix, giving her a gourd. He and Obelix tried to tell her, in sign language, exactly what it would do – and when they gave Dogmatix a tiny sip, and he showed how he could kick huge boulders into the air and then catch them on his nose, she obviously got the idea. Then they drove on along Watling Street towards Viroconium.

Remove a MAGIC POTION CARD from ASTERIX'S WAIST-SLIT. Now go to 38.

273

It certainly seemed hard on Dogmatix not to let him stretch his legs after the sea crossing, so the Gauls waited on the banks of the Tamesis for a time, while he chased happily about. But he couldn't seem to catch any menhirs, let alone rabbits – or even better, boars – and so in the end Asterix said they really ought to be moving on. In fact, it turned out to have been a mistake to wait about so long, because they suddenly heard the noise of oars behind them, and turned to see a large Roman galley which had come up the mouth of the river. Men for the garrison of Londinium were disembarking. 'Here!' shouted their centurion, seeing two non-Romans out after dark, which was against the rules. 'What are you two doing?' 'Er – just walking the dog!' said Asterix. Dogmatix came chasing along to back up this story. 'Got permission to walk the dog after dark, have you?' asked the centurion. 'Of course!' said Asterix. 'Right – then you can tell me the password you need for dog-walking!' the centurion said.

Is OBELIX carrying a PASSWORD SCROLL? If so, use it to find out the correct password by placing it exactly over the scroll shape below – then follow the appropriate instruction. If not, you must guess which instruction to follow.

```
        A     S   W   A
           N  GI D   A
        M     A       M Y
         SU      N      S
        H  I   O   E    S
         E        A S
        T   !7    A    N D
          6 9     B      L O
        O M        E   T  R
```

If you think it's GOAT	go to 111
If you think it's RAM	go to 266
If you think it's STAG	go to 101

'*OATS*!' said Obelix, preparing to stride past the Roman patrol. 'Oh no, it isn't!' said the decurion. 'Wrong password . . . and now I come to look at you two, we've all got orders to arrest a titchy little Gaul and a great big fat one! Seize them!' he told his men. 'What do you mean, fat?' asked the furious Obelix, wading into the Romans. As the decurion yelled for reinforcements, Asterix realised they risked being delayed at the very start of their mission. He drank some magic potion, and went to help Obelix wipe up the Romans. Soon they were strolling down to the beach, where they hired a little jolly-boat from a friendly Gaul called Aquatix.

Remove a *MAGIC POTION CARD* from *ASTERIX'S WAIST-SLIT*. Go to 51.

'Yes, the password is *MISTLETOE*!' said the druid, suddenly becoming very genial. 'I see you are genuine seekers after the truth, after all!' 'Actually, we're genuine seekers after mistletoe,' said Asterix, and explained all about Operation Britain. 'And the best of luck to you!' said the druid. 'Your best route is to go from here to Deva – thus avoiding the mountains – and then on round the coastline. Here, take this bag of coins! I'm only too happy to do what I can to help you and your Gaulish druid!' 'Thank you,' said Asterix, getting into the chariot with Obelix and Dogmatix. 'Well, off we go to Deva!'

If OBELIX is not already carrying the COINBAG, put it in his WAIST-SLIT. Now go to 153.

276

Next morning they set off for Londinium, which Asterix thought was the best bet. 'Not many Romans about the roads this morning,' he noticed, as they went along. 'Their defeat yesterday must have given them a nasty shock!' About halfway to Londinium, however, they came to a roadblock manned not by Romans, but by Britons – the fort beyond it seemed to be full of Britons too. Asterix and Obelix explained their quest, but the Britons did not seem to have heard of them, and were rather suspicious. 'You *say* that you've been fighting in Cantium, but we wouldn't know anything about that,' they said. 'We're Iceni, from further north. Can you give us the password?'

Is OBELIX carrying a PASSWORD SCROLL? If so, find out the correct password by placing it exactly over the scroll shape on the next page, and then follow the appropriate instruction. If not, you'll have to choose which instruction to follow.

```
   L    A    R    AI
        S   B O       N
        D        U    PL
       USE       F    OR
  T     E   ST        T
        E   U    J
        OU       R S
        LA   M E R I
  LL    E    U    R
```

If you think it's BEER   go to 170
If you think it's MEAD   go to 19
If you think it's WINE   go to 70

277

Without a translator, the Gauls couldn't make out what the butcher was saying – but he made his meaning clear by pointing to the road they ought to take, and they set off again. Every now and then they saw a few Romans in the distance, but it was easy enough to avoid them. (Obelix didn't really want to avoid them, but Asterix insisted that they must hurry on to Anticlimax's village – and he didn't want to use up his own supplies of magic potion except in real emergency.) Not only did Dogmatix get a second bone, the butcher had insisted on handing Obelix and Asterix some nice pork-pies to eat. 'Not up to a real roast boar, but better than nothing,' said Obelix, enjoying his as they went along. 'I hope we soon find a place to stop for the night and get a good meal, though.' *Go to 109.*

'It's a pity we couldn't understand what the foreign seaman was saying,' said Asterix, as Ekonomikrisis sailed away from the Roman patrol ship towards the British coast. 'We'll just have to trust to luck.' 'Here comes some luck!' said Obelix happily, as a familiar vessel flying the skull and crossbones hove in sight. 'The pirates! Oh, won't they be pleased to see us!' Asterix was not nearly as glad to see the pirates as Obelix – it all meant more delay, and Operation Britain was urgent! But he couldn't bear to deprive Obelix of the treat of a reunion with their old friends, though in the end, as the fun of the sea battle seemed to be going on rather a long time, he decided to take a magic potion and scuttle the pirate ship himself. Now they could sail on and put in at the first big port they came to on the British coast.

Remove a *MAGIC POTION CARD* from *ASTERIX'S WAIST-SLIT. Now go to 142.*

'Yes, I'm sure this was the road to choose!' said Asterix. 'The sun is sinking low, and I can tell we're making back towards Cantium.' It was a good, well-made, Roman road too. But all of a sudden, they turned a corner and ran straight into a good, well-made, Roman roadblock. 'Halt!' shouted the decurion in command of the roadblock. 'This road is closed to unauthorised travellers – all the ports are being watched for two dangerous Gauls reported to be crossing the Mare Britannicum. Not you, by any chance?' he added, peering closely at the Gauls. 'No, no, we're not a bit dangerous,' Asterix assured him. 'As you can see, I'm much too small to hurt anyone – and big as my friend there may be, he wouldn't hurt a fly!' 'Then prove your credentials by giving the password,' said the decurion.

Is OBELIX carrying a PASSWORD SCROLL? If so, use it to find out the correct password by placing it exactly over the scroll shape below, and then follow the appropriate instruction. If not, you must guess which instruction to follow.

```
IP    S    O    FA

C    T  CO      A

N    I  M  L AC

!  R  A    C  K  R

S  P  U        D E

   E    FO L      I

     I A  TU     E

7    6 S  DO    G

  L    I    C E   N

        C       E
```

If you think it's CAESAR	go to 96
If you think it's CLAUDIUS	go to 130
If you think it's HADRIAN	go to 269

They decided to try going towards Glevum, and after driving their chariot down the Fosse Way in that direction for a little while, they stopped at a typical British pub for a typical British warm beer, since there was nothing else to be had. The landlord, a cheery soul, got into conversation with them. Asterix made out they were tourists seeing the sights of Britain. 'And now you're off towards Glevum, eh?' said the landlord. 'Well, carry on a bit farther and you'll reach the mouth of the Sabrina river. You might even see the Severn Bore.' 'Seven boar?' said Obelix, coming over all excited. 'Goody, goody!' 'Is that on the way to Mona?' asked Asterix. 'Mona? Oh, dear me, no. Mona is in the other direction!' said the landlord. 'You should have gone to Viroconium, not Glevum, if you want to see Mona.' 'Come along, Obelix,' said Asterix, leaving the pub. 'We must turn back.' 'But I want to see the seven boar! We might even catch one or two of them!' protested Obelix. 'There *is* only one, and it's a tidal wave,' Asterix explained. 'We must make for Viroconium.' *Go to 38.*

'Let's try the road to Calleva,' said Asterix. They went along it for a little while, but then they met a Briton and stopped to ask him the way. 'Calleva? Oh no, that's nowhere near Londinium,' said the man. 'You ought to have started out in the direction of Durobrivae.' 'Too bad,' said Asterix. 'Well, let's go back to that signpost and try again.' *Go to 116.*

Since Obelix had no password scroll, he simply had to guess. 'Wrong!' said the centurion. 'It's not *GOAT*! Here, you, Tedius!' he told a passing legionary. 'I can't leave my post, but you run off and find Centurion Outrageous. Tell him there's a great fat Gaul asking for military information, just like that – and naturally he doesn't know the password! Eek!' he added with a screech of terror as Obelix, infuriated by being called fat, picked him up by the scruff of his neck and shook him vigorously. 'Obelix! Put him down!' said Asterix, at just the same moment as the centurion and a large troop of legionaries appeared. Obelix looked ready to tackle the lot of them, but Asterix thought this was no time to get involved in a long battle. He drank some magic potion, rushed into the fray, and hauled his friend out of it. 'I hadn't finished!' said the indignant Obelix. 'I dare say not,' said Asterix, 'but we want information, not a punch-up! Come on, Obelix. Let's walk round the outside of the barracks.'

Remove a MAGIC POTION CARD from ASTERIX'S WAIST-SLIT. Now go to 11.

283

The Gauls had no money left to pay the toll for crossing the bridge – and they feared the Romans would be after them by now, so there was no time to be lost. When they tried to force their way past the collector, however, he called a squad of Roman soldiers to his aid. Asterix drank a magic potion. 'You throw half of them in the river that side of the bridge, and I'll throw the others in this side!' he told Obelix. They finished crossing the bridge to the sound of much splashing and swearing from the Roman soldiers as they floundered in the waters of the river Tamesis. 'I think our next port of call should be the Governor's palace,' said Asterix. 'Let's try it!'

Remove a MAGIC POTION CARD from ASTERIX'S WAIST-SLIT. Now go to 2. (Remember: when there are no magic potion cards left in Asterix's waist-slit, Operation Britain cannot go on, and you must start the game again.)

Asterix approached the fishmonger. 'And what can I do for you?' asked the fishmonger. 'We'll have some of whatever's fresh – lots of it!' said Asterix, thinking of Obelix's appetite. 'And another thing; can you give us any information about the movement of Roman troops over the countryside? We're friends of Anticlimax – in fact he's my cousin.' 'Hm,' said Fishcax, thoughtfully. 'You may *say* you're friends of his – but how do I know you're telling the truth? Can you give me the secret resistance password?'

Is OBELIX carrying a PASSWORD SCROLL? If so, find out the correct password by placing it exactly over the scroll shape below. Then follow the appropriate instruction. If not, you must guess which instruction to follow.

```
A     R     B     RE
  DM  E     NO  I  E
 L   LA    US    EI
LL     TE      SC
OLL      LI   GE
 A      RC  H    I
T    Y  PT  EA
  LO     B      O
 T        O   M E
```

If you think it's MISTLETOE	go to 252
If you think it's PARSLEY	go to 47
If you think it's THYME	go to 5